Other books by this author

Two Centuries of Panic: A History of Corporate Collapses in Australia

The Bold Riders: Behind Australia's Corporate Collapses

The Money Miners: The Great Australian Mining Boom

Operation Dynasty: How Warwick Took Fairfax

Vintage Pierpont

The Official History of Blue Sky Mines

To my sister Elaine, in deep gratitude for the support she and her husband Kevin have given our family

First published in 2001
Reprinted 2003
Copyright © Trevor Sykes 2001, 2003

All rights reserved. No part of this book may be reproduced or transmitted in any form or by any means, electronic or mechanical, including photocopying, recording or by any information storage and retrieval system, without prior permission in writing from the publisher. *The Australian Copyright Act 1968* (the Act) allows a maximum of one chapter or 10 per cent of this book, whichever is the greater, to be photocopied by any educational institution for its educational purposes provided that the educational institution (or body that administers it) has given a remuneration notice to Copyright Agency Limited (CAL) under the Act.

Allen & Unwin
83 Alexander Street
Crows Nest NSW 2065
Australia
Phone: (61 2) 8425 0100
Fax: (61 2) 9906 2218
Email: frontdesk@allen-unwin.com.au
Web: http://www.allenandunwin.com

National Library of Australia
Cataloguing-in-Publication entry:

Sykes, Trevor.
  The numbers game.

  2nd ed.
  Includes index.
  ISBN 1 174114 294 6.

  1. Investments. I. Title.

332.678

Set in 10.5/13 pt Janson by Midland Typesetters
Printed by Griffin Press, South Australia
10 9 8 7 6 5 4 3 2 1

The Numbers Game

2nd edition

TREVOR SYKES

Contents

Figures and tables		v
Acronyms		vii
Thanks		ix
Introduction		x
1	**Investment basics**	**1**
	Financial experts • Investment strategy	
	• The end game	
2	**Basic analysis**	**14**
	The annual report • The profit and loss account	
	• The balance sheet • The cash flow statement	
3	**Types of companies**	**42**
	TMT companies • Retailers • Gaming companies	
	• Insurance companies • Banks • Mining companies	
	• Oil and gas companies	
4	**Managed investments**	**132**
	Funds • Property trusts	
5	**Prospectuses**	**141**
	Analysis	
6	**Takeovers**	**152**
	Hostile bids • Friendly bids • Loyalty	
7	**A few danger signals**	**157**
8	**Fixed interest**	**165**
	The inverse correlation • Who is the guarantor?	
	• Ratings	
Epilogue		173
Notes		174
Index		178

Figures and tables

Figures

3.1	Value of one year's new business—insurance operations	68
5.1	The hockey stick	150

Tables

1.1	Me and Mrs Jones: Profile of a trailing commission	7
1.2	Best investments year by year 1988–98	11
1.3	How many years will your money last?	12
2.1	Amcor's profit, 1998–99	17
2.2	Amcor over six years	23
2.3	Amcor's balance sheet, 1998–99	26
2.4	Amcor's cash flow statement, year to 30 June 1999	38
2.5	Digicall cash flow, six months to December 1995	39
3.1	Coles Myer profit-to-sales analysis	51
3.2	Coles Myer stock-turn ratio	52
3.3	Coles Myer sales per square metre	53
3.4	AMP balance sheet, 31 December 1999	61
3.5	Calculating the value of AMP's liabilities, 1999	62
3.6	Insurance company discount rates	64
3.7	MoS shareholder profit analysis	70
3.8	AMP Life statutory funds' embedded value, 1999	71
3.9	Colonial group solvency reserves, 1999	72
3.10	HIH balance sheet, June 2000	79
3.11	Adjustments to HIH's 2000 balance sheet	83
3.12	GIO segmental information	87

vi THE NUMBERS GAME

3.13	Westpac profit and loss, 30 September 1999	90
3.14	Westpac balance sheet, 30 September 1999	91
3.15	Key Westpac numbers and ratios	94
3.16	Westpac's non-accruals	97
3.17	Westpac's free capital, parent company accounts	97
3.18	Westpac interest rate risk, 1999	99
3.19	Westpac trading derivatives outstanding, 30 September 1999	101
3.20	Importer's gains or losses	102
4.1	Largest Australian share funds as at 19 May 2003	136
4.2	Average management expense ratios, 2003	138
5.1	ChaosMusic prospectus (indicated capital structure)	146
5.2	ChaosMusic pro forma balance sheet (projections for 30 June 1999)	146
5.3	Silver Rose proposed float	148
7.1	Summary of Chase Corporation's balance sheet, 1988	161
7.2	Profit and loss account for CSR, 1984	162
7.3	CSR's 1984 extraordinaries	163
8.1	Australian interest rates 1976–99	167

Acronyms

AASB	Australian Accounting Standards Board
ASX	Australian Stock Exchange
B2C operations	business-to-consumer operations
CRA	Conzinc Riotinto of Australia
D&A	depreciation and amortisation
DCF	discounted cash flow
DPS	dividends per share
DRIP	dividend reinvestment plan
E	earnings
EBIT	earnings before interest and tax
EBITDA	earnings before interest, tax, depreciation and amortisation
EPS	earnings per share
IBNER	incurred but not enough reported
IBNR	incurred but not reported
MER	management expense ratio
MoS	margin on services
NAB	net asset backing
NCSC	National Corporations and Securities Commission
NPAT	net profit after tax
NPV	net present value
P&L account	profit and loss account
P/E multiple	price/earnings multiple (or ratio)
P/EBIT multiple	price/earnings before interest and tax multiple

vii

viii THE NUMBERS GAME

P/EBITDA multiple	price/earnings before interest, tax, depreciation and amortisation multiple
P/EBITDAM multiple	price/earnings before interest, tax, depreciation, amortisation and marketing cost multiple
P/R multiple	price/revenue multiple
PBL	Publishing & Broadcasting Limited
PBT	profit before tax
PPE	property, plant and equipment
RAB	rotary air blast
RC drilling	reverse circulation drilling
ROA	return on assets
SRE	single responsible entity
TMT stock	telcos, media and technology stock
WMC	Western Mining Corporation

Thanks

The best way of discovering how ignorant you are of any subject is to attempt to write a quasi textbook on it. After my persistent publisher Patrick Gallagher had finally succeeded in beseeching me to write this book, I quickly discovered that my largely self-taught skills in balance sheet analysis had a number of gaps. The remedy was a generous lunching program for friends whose technical abilities and experience were greater than mine. The errors and prejudices in this book remain mine, but I would like to pay tribute to various books and people who helped on technical issues.

On accounting principles, my bible is *Guide to Accounting Standards* by J.B. and M.A. Shanahan (Deloitte Touche Tohmatsu, 1997). Accounting standards in Australia have become a movable feast, so the Shanahans' tome has to be revised annually. It is invaluable to anyone who wants to keep up to speed. On mining and oil stocks, my guide is Dr Victor Rudenno's *The Mining Valuation Handbook* (Wrightbooks, 1998). I borrowed from it extensively for the chapter on oil stocks.

I am deeply grateful to several experts and friends for technical advice, including John Phillips (former deputy governor of the Reserve Bank of Australia) on banking; David Goodsall (director of actuarial services, Ernst & Young) on insurance; Lily Kwong (gaming analyst, Deutsche Bank) on gaming stocks; and Tony Lewis (of Lewis Securities) on fixed interest. If any facts managed to sneak into this book, they are responsible. The opinions are entirely mine.

Introduction

Look at a maritime chart of the coastal seas around Australia and you will see a host of names such as Smith's Rock, Robinson's Reef and Brown's Shoal. All these features were discovered unintentionally. Smith, Robinson and Brown got their names onto the chart by being the skippers of ships that ran into these rocks, reefs and shoals.

This book is Sykes' chart of Australian balance sheet analysis and has been compiled in much the same unintentional way. As a finance writer and occasional investor over many decades, I have hit or seen almost every rock, reef and shoal in the investment world. In the process I have developed a number of prejudices, which the reader will see as we go along. *The Numbers Game* is very much a collection of personal views and biases and is endorsed by absolutely nobody in authority.

But if it helps the reader avoid a single shoal, it will have covered its purchase price.

1

Investment basics

The two fundamental ways of investing in financial markets are by being an owner or a lender.

Anyone who invests in a share in the Commonwealth Bank becomes a part-owner of it. Anyone who invests in a term deposit with the bank becomes a lender to it.

Lenders have more security than owners. If a company goes into liquidation, the assets are distributed amongst its stakeholders in the following order:

1 Liquidator's fees and legal expenses
2 Employees' wages, holiday pay, long service leave and redundancy
3 Secured creditors, including debenture holders
4 Unsecured creditors, including the Australian Taxation Office
5 Preference shareholders
6 Ordinary shareholders

The higher you rank up this chain, the better your chances of being paid out.[1] After all debtors have been paid what they are owed and the preference shareholders have been repaid their capital and any accrued dividends, the ordinary shareholders divide whatever is left in the kitty. In practice, when a company goes bust it frequently doesn't have enough to even pay its unsecured creditors, so ordinary shareholders almost never get a cent. In former days they were at least left with scrip certificates which they could use as wallpaper, but in these days of computer printouts they don't even have that small asset.

1

2 THE NUMBERS GAME

Secured creditors have more protection, and indeed enjoy a little more protection than would appear from their position on the list. A bank, for example, may have a mortgage for $10 million over the company's head office, secured by a registered charge. In the event of the company collapsing, the bank can appoint a receiver to seize the building and sell it. If the receiver gets $10 million for the building, the bank is out square. If the receiver gets $11 million, he pays the bank its $10 million and returns the other $1 million (less his fees) to the liquidator of the company. If the receiver gets only $9 million for the building, the bank gets that money and becomes an unsecured creditor for the remaining $1 million.

Debenture holders are secured in the same fashion. A debenture is secured by a trust deed, normally over all the assets of the company that are not otherwise mortgaged. When the company collapses, the trustee can appoint a receiver on behalf of the debenture holders. The receiver will then have control of all the assets of the company and the liquidator will have very little to do.

Noteholders are normally unsecured lenders to the company. Their status in the ranking on liquidation will depend on the terms of the trust deed, but often they are lumped in with unsecured creditors.

So if a company collapses, it is better to be a debenture holder than a noteholder and it's better to be a noteholder than a shareholder.

The list also illustrates neatly the risk–reward paradigm that underlies corporate financing. The stakeholders who take the least risk get the lowest rewards. A secured lender might earn 6 per cent on a debenture while the holder of an unsecured note might earn 7 per cent. If the company strikes a bonanza that's still all they earn. The bonanza will, in theory anyway, be reaped by the shareholders (equity holders, if you prefer). On the other hand, if the company goes bust the shares become worthless but the lenders have a little more protection. As we have noted, that's the theory. It doesn't always work out that way in practice when a company goes belly-up.

Preference shares come in a Heinz range of varieties. A plain vanilla pref gets a secured dividend which must be paid before ordinary shareholders are entitled to a dividend. The pref shareholder also ranks for payout ahead of the ordinary shareholders in a liquidation.

But pref shares have quite a few permutations and it's worth examining exactly what bells and whistles are attached before buying them. They may come with variable rights to dividend, which means that the dividend may rise and fall a little depending on the performance of the company. They may be redeemable, which means the company can buy them back at specified times and prices. They may be convertible, which means that they carry the right at some future date to convert into ordinary shares on specified terms. They may be cumulative, which means that if a dividend is not paid it accumulates. If a company cannot pay its 8 per cent (say) dividend on the prefs in a given year, then the rights to the dividend accumulate until it does pay. And normally those dividends would have to be paid before any dividends could be paid on ordinary shares. So now you know what it means when the share tables in the morning paper talk about a cum. conv. red. pref. (cumulative, convertible, redeemable, preference) share.

Sometimes a pref share may be non-cumulative, which means that once a dividend is passed it's gone forever. The terms of some modern hybrid securities include a provision that if a pref dividend is passed (not paid), then the company may not pay a dividend on the prefs until all arrears of pref divs have been restored. This, of course, is better than losing a pref div forever. And it's one more good reason for always checking the fine print of the terms upon which hybrids are issued.

PREJUDICE 1

Non-cumulative pref shares are a fairly poor investment. Why buy prefs in a company that isn't confident it can maintain the dividends on them?

Which leads to another thought. An investment in debentures, notes or pref shares should be made for the purpose of receiving fixed income. These investments should not be made on the grounds that they will be more secure if the company goes broke. It is pretty dumb to invest in a company where a

4 THE NUMBERS GAME

risk is perceived that it might go down the tubes. It doesn't matter where you rank on the above list: if the company goes belly-up, the Australian legal system will ensure you will have to wait years to get your money back—if you get it back at all.

How do you know if a company might go belly-up? Analysis of the annual report might just help. But before we start on that, a word or two about experts and strategy.

Financial experts

If you don't know anyone smarter than yourself, you'd better read this.

There are four ways of betting on racehorses. One is by following tips from an expert, another is by studying the form. Or you can do both: listen to an expert and then check the form. Or finally, you can just punt on any horse that takes your fancy.

Similarly, there are four ways of investing. One is by following tips from an expert. The financial sector is crammed with highly paid (and too often overpaid) people who make their living by claiming to be investment experts. All of them will claim to be the answer to your prayers. In truth, they bunch like a scatter graph. A few are excellent, quite a few are good, most are medium and some are crooks and charlatans.

Investors should be aware that at any given time there are a number of shysters around Australia peddling get-rich-quick schemes. Typically offers were being sent out unsolicited in the mail, offering to make their customers wealthy by setting them up in tax havens or selling them share trading systems or racing systems or whatever. Anyone receiving tempting literature like this should just ask themselves one simple question: If these roosters really know how to make millions, why are they offering to sell me their secrets? Unsolicited?

Anyone who falls for offers like those is probably beyond help. The rest of us need a little help and it's available from financial advisors. This is an area where the Australian Securities & Investments Commission (ASIC) can be helpful. They provide a short, easily understood handbook to guide investors in their choice of financial advisors. They also list licensed advisors on their website. That's well worth checking, because anyone claiming to be an advisor who isn't on that list can be crossed off without further checking.[2] Check around your friends, neighbours and workmates to find out who has used financial advisors and, importantly, for how long. If they've had a bad experience with an advisor, cross that one off your list immediately. The longer they've known a good advisor and the more highly they commend him or her, the better.

The big trick in investment is to find smart people. If you can find just one, then stop reading and give this book to your worst enemy because you don't need to read it any more.

Advisors

Sorting good financial advisors from bad ones is difficult enough for seasoned investors and nearly impossible for a novice. The most important point to remember when interviewing a financial advisor is that this is no time for diffidence. Your life savings may be at stake. Don't be embarrassed to show ignorance of financial complexities. If anything isn't clear, ask questions, and don't stop asking until you're quite satisfied you understand the answer. If the advisor is vague or supercilious, scrub them off your list and just walk out. Millions of dollars have been lost by novice investors who didn't. However, even a novice can sort them out to some extent at the first meeting by asking three questions.

Question 1: Who pays them? If Leo Liability the sharebroker buys shares for a client, he will send out a contract note afterwards showing the cost of the stock plus the cost of his commission. If Leo were acting as a financial advisor whom you consult before investing your nest egg, he should charge you a commission for that service in just the same way. If your financial advisor doesn't charge you a commission, that means he is getting it from somewhere else. He's not working for free.

By law in Australia, before financial advisors invest a cent of your money they should:

1 provide documentation on who they are and what their qualifications are, including their licence number;

6 THE NUMBERS GAME

2 spend some time talking to the client to discover the appropriate investments (guaranteed income for a retiree, a bit of risk for a young executive);

3 provide a written 'customer advice record' setting out their advice and recommendations to the client;

4 disclose any association with investments they recommend (if the advisor's firm is owned by, say, Mercantile Mutual, and the advisor is recommending one of Mercantile Mutual's funds, the association should be disclosed);

5 get the client's signed consent to the proposed investment before making the investment; and

6 disclose any commissions they will earn from the proposed investments.

These various disclosures have been compelled following the disasters of the 1980s when some financial advisors gave advice to their clients that was downright criminal. Brokers and financial advisors now have a duty to 'know the client', so that they are in a position to give him or her the appropriate advice.

All of this generates some paperwork but is aimed at preventing the downright frauds committed by some financial advisors on their clients in the 1980s. In those years, several financial advisors steered their clients into the fraudulent Estate Mortgage group of trusts because Estate Mortgage kicked back the highest commissions to the financial advisors. The advisors therefore had an incentive to shove their clients into whichever outfit paid them the highest commissions, regardless of the merits of the investment. Maybe the advisors didn't know that the trusts were fraudulent, but they didn't bother to research them much either. After Estate Mortgage collapsed, horror stories began to emerge of widows who had been advised to put their entire legacy into Estate Mortgage. Even if Estate Mortgage had been sound it would have been risky policy to put all your eggs in the one basket. The very fact that Estate Mortgage was offering the highest commissions around should have been a danger signal to even a fairly slack financial advisor.

Whatever investments are being recommended, it is far better in principle that the advisor gets commissions from the client so that the advisor's wealth grows with the client's and therefore the advisor has a vested interest in the client's success. It also means the advisor should be able to take an objective view about investments. The advisor might still be wrong, but at least he or she will be objective.

If your advisor is insulted when you ask who pays him or her, start looking for someone else straight away. And remember the advisor should provide all the disclosures listed above. As advisors collect their commissions in different ways, be sure you understand all of them, and how much they will cost. Probably the most important to understand is the trailing commission. The trailing commission is the one levied on the total amount of your investment and varies between 0.25 per cent and 1 per cent a year. It doesn't sound much, but it compounds to your disadvantage. Let's assume Widow Jones has gone to a financial advisor with a $100 000 inheritance and he has invested it in a group of funds which will average 5 per cent annual return over the next 10 years.

Table 1.1 Me and Mrs Jones
Profile of a trailing commission

Initial investment	Time	Average return	Gross return amount	Trailing commission rate	Trailing commission amount	Net return
$100 000	10 yrs	5%	$160 678	0.75%	$9 329	$151 349
$100 000	10 yrs	5%	$160 678	1.00%	$12 292	$147 669

Source: ASIC[3]

To begin with, advisors will always claim they're going to do heaps better than 5 per cent, but it's amazing how few don't— especially in the lean times between 2001 and 2003.

So 5 per cent is not an unfair rate, but you can adjust the calculation to 7 per cent return if you like. It doesn't really matter, because arithmetically the relationship between the average earning rate and the trailing commission will stay the same, because the trailing commission is calculated on the gross value of your assets and the advisor will hence take a bigger slice if the portfolio grows at a faster rate. Incidentally, if you've struck an advisor who can regularly, year after year, do 10 per cent or better, marry them.

8 THE NUMBERS GAME

At 0.75 per cent, the trailing commission has chewed up 15 per cent of Widow Jones' earnings over the decade. At 1 per cent, it has eaten more than 20 per cent. So that innocent-looking 1 per cent trail will gobble $1 in every $5 that the fund managers manage to earn. It gets worse if the fund managers actually lose some of your money, because the advisor is still getting his commission on the gross.

If Widow Jones wandered into an institution and offered to buy, say, an insurance bond with her $100 000, she might well have been given an alternative. The institution might have told her that she would have to pay 3 per cent up-front, but that a financial advisor could get it for her for 1 per cent. But the 1 per cent is a trail, which we've already seen. By having the 3 per cent deducted at first, Widow Jones is really only investing $97 000. But after 10 years at 5 per cent average growth she would have $158 000, which is less than the gross return she would have achieved in Table 1.1 but considerably better than her net after the advisor had sucked out his trailing commission.

The above example, far from incidentally, takes no cognisance of any other fees that may be levied on Widow Jones. She should add them all up and do the arithmetic, or find a kindly friend who will do it for her, before she commits to the advisor.

It should be noted that in practice, the example would never work out this neatly. One reason is because performance is erratic. The performance in the first couple of years of the investment will have a dramatic effect on its performance over the remainder. Another factor that can affect the result is the timing and frequency of the trailing commission—whether it's imposed annually or quarterly and whether it's imposed at the start or finish of the periods. The more frequently it is imposed and the earlier, the worse it is for the client.

PREJUDICE 2

A trailing commission is a thief in the night, returning to pirate your nest egg year after year without any relationship to the quality of advice given.

Question 2: Does your advisor have professional indemnity insurance? If the advisor doesn't, and proves incompetent or crooked, you may have little chance of retrieving anything from the subsequent wreckage. While on this point, make sure you keep all your paperwork. A complete paper trail is crucial if you ever want to trace an advisor's mistakes or misdeeds.

Question 3: Does your advisor ever make investment mistakes?

In the movie *Ten*, Bo Derek rated ten out of ten for being the perfect woman. In the investment world there aren't any Bo Dereks.

For every investor who loses money at the hands of a criminal advisor, there must be 99 who suffer because their advisor is honest but ordinary. An expert, by my standards, is anyone who can get six investment recommendations right out of ten. None of them can get ten out of ten, and you should be able to get five out of ten by throwing darts at the share list. An investment advisor who says he never makes mistakes is either deluded or lying.

Try to get advice from more than one advisor, and follow their tips over time. You will probably find there are horses for courses. One may be good at fixed interest, another at overall investment strategy, a third at speculative stocks and so on.

Alan Cameron, chairman of the Australian Securities & Investments Commission (ASIC), once described a professional investor as someone who had already lost money. It's one of the smartest things Alan ever said. Investors learn a lot more from their mistakes than their successes.

PREJUDICE 3

Judge financial advisors by their scalps. If any grey hairs can be seen, they've been around long enough to have seen a few market cycles. With any luck, they've already made their mistakes at someone else's expense. The bright kids haven't made their mistakes yet.

10   THE NUMBERS GAME

As pointed out before, if you can find smart people you don't need to read this book any further. Otherwise you are going to have to learn at least enough to make you comfortable with investment jargon and hopefully enough for you to be able to evaluate the advice you're being given.

Let's start with the big picture: investment strategy.

Investment strategy

If all the markets always stayed the same, there would be one perfect investment strategy. They don't, so there isn't.

The classic advice is not to put all your eggs in one basket. Actually if anyone were capable of choosing the right basket every time, this would be the best possible strategy. But it would also be equivalent to buying the winning ticket in every lottery, so for ordinary mortals it's safer to diversify.

Professional investors argue forever over what is the ideal investment mix. The truth is that it varies as markets vary and even the professionals never get it right.

The classic mix used to be one-third fixed interest, one-third equities and one-third property. This is still a very useful default, particularly for small investors. If the portfolio is not mixed that way, why not? Sometimes there's a good argument and sometimes there isn't.

Since the A$ floated and became freely convertible, there is quite a valid argument that a proportion of a portfolio ought to be in foreign securities. Table 1.2 was produced by InTech Research. It shows how various classes of financial assets had performed in the previous decade. The message is very clear. Every dog has his day and so does every asset category.

The correct weighting of such a portfolio is open to argument but on balance it would probably be something like:

- Australian equities, 30 per cent;
- international equities, 20 per cent;
- property trusts, 15 per cent;
- fixed interest, 30 per cent; and
- cash, 5 per cent.

INVESTMENT BASICS **11**

Table 1.2 Best investments year by year 1988–98 (shown in annual percentage gains or losses)

	Australian shares	International shares	Listed property trusts	Australian fixed interest	Cash
1990	(17.5)	(15.1)	8.7	**19.1**	16.1
1991	**34.2**	20.0	20.1	24.7	11.2
1992	(2.3)	4.9	7.0	**10.4**	6.9
1993	**45.4**	23.8	30.1	16.3	5.4
1994	(8.7)	(8.1)	(5.6)	(4.7)	**5.4**
1995	20.2	**26.0**	12.7	18.6	8.0
1996	**14.6**	6.2	14.5	11.9	7.6
1997	12.2	**41.6**	20.3	12.2	5.6
1998	11.6	**32.3**	18.0	9.5	5.1
1999	16.1	**17.2**	(5.0)	(1.2)	5.0
2000	5.2	2.2	**17.8**	12.1	6.3
2001	10.4	(10.0)	**14.6**	5.4	5.2
2002	(8.8)	(27.4)	**11.8**	8.8	4.8

Source: InTech Research

More important than the actual weightings is the discipline of rebalancing every year or half-year. Say an investor was working on the above weightings. In 1993 that investor would have found that because Australian shares were rising in value faster than any other category they might have gone from 30 to 40 per cent of the portfolio. Meanwhile, because international shares had under-performed that year, they might have fallen from 20 per cent to 12 per cent. In those circumstances, the investor would have rebalanced by selling some Australian equities and investing more in international equities.

Rebalancing is not by itself a magic solution. Like every mechanistic device, it needs to be interpreted with a little common sense. After the tech crash of 2000, when the $US was also looking very toppy, few investors would have kept reinvesting fully in international shares, particularly American.

Rebalancing automatically means that an investor is selling out of the hottest sector in the portfolio and investing in the under-performing sectors. This makes sense, because no category outperforms the others indefinitely, even though it might for a few years.

The more money someone has to invest, the further they can diversify. If someone is starting with very little, it's probably safest to stick to Australian investments. After all, if you don't understand what you're doing in your own market, you're not likely to have much chance anywhere else.

The important point is to have a portfolio mix and to stick with it. The discipline of doing this will stop you from plunging the lot on mining stocks or Internet shares or whatever the fashionable gambling chips of the day happen to be.

The end game

Before leaving the subject of investment strategy, let's consider the end game for a second. One of the most frequently asked questions in investment is: How much money do I need to retire? The answer depends on two factors: your cost of living and the amount you earn on your investments. Table 1.3, from BT Funds Management, provides a very useful guide.

Table 1.3 How many years will your money last?

Net earning rate (%)	Rate of withdrawal of capital (%)										
	6	7	8	9	10	11	12	13	14	15	16
12							26	19	15	13	11
11						29	20	16	14	12	11
10					33	22	17	14	12	11	10
9				37	23	18	15	13	12	10	9
8			43	26	20	16	14	12	11	10	9
7		51	28	21	17	15	13	11	10	9	9
6	61	31	23	18	16	13	12	11	10	9	8
5	35	25	20	17	14	13	11	10	9	9	8

Source: BT Funds Management

The table demonstrates that if a widow is withdrawing capital from her portfolio at the rate of 11 per cent a year and the portfolio is earning at the rate of 10 per cent, her nest egg will last 22 years. If her earning rate drops to 6 per cent, however, it will last only thirteen years.

If she wants to get more cold-blooded about the equation, she can calculate how long she has left to live. If it's twenty years, the table tells us she can afford to withdraw capital only at 1 or 2 per cent above her earning rate. If she's going to live a long time and wants to leave a legacy, she can't afford to withdraw much above her earning rate at all. A grim calculation, but one that too few people do.

The table is an illustration of the power of compound interest, and the rate at which it can erode capital. It also indicates that capital is more easily retained if the withdrawal rate is low. A retiree withdrawing capital at the rate of 9 per cent a year will exhaust capital in seventeen years if it is only earning 5 per cent. That's a 4 per cent gap between the withdrawal and earning rate. However, if the withdrawal rate rises to 15 per cent and the earning rate to 11 per cent, the money will go in twelve years, although the gap is still only 4 per cent. Which explains why the old tend to be thrifty.

2

Basic analysis

The annual report

By law, every listed company in Australia has to produce an annual report, telling investors what it does, who its directors are and how it has performed, and a set of accounts which include its profit and loss account, balance sheet, cash flow statement and notes to the accounts.

It's worth checking the last annual report. Most companies of any size now have their annual reports available on the Internet. Those that don't should be able to supply a copy to any intending investor who telephones them. If the company won't or can't supply an annual report, scratch it off your list.

When you get the report, the first point worth checking is the date the accounts were signed off (look at the bottom of the auditor's statement). If a company cannot get its annual report out within four months of balance date it is either inefficient or is undergoing legal or auditing problems. So if a company that balances on 30 June can't get its annual report out before the end of October you're safer ignoring it unless you have a very good reason to do otherwise.

Read the annual report. Do you understand what the company does? Does it seem to be doing it well? Even more importantly, do the directors seem to have a good track record in the industry?

If the answers are yes, yes and yes, let's go through to the financials.

14

The profit and loss account (in modern jargon, the performance statement)

The annual report can be divided into two halves. The first half is written in English (more or less) and describes what the company does for a living. The second half comprises the accounts, sometimes called the Chinese section because the numbers run vertically, and tells whether the company is really making a living.

Or rather, *should* tell. The oldest saying in finance is that figures don't lie, but liars can figure. The figures in the accounts may be the unvarnished truth or they may be a carefully painted picture. If a company is really determined to lie about its position and the auditors are too stupid or corrupt to correct them, then an investor has only a poor chance of detecting it. But if the accounts are even roughly honest, the investor should be able to read the health of the company from a few vital signs.

The accounts may be divided into four parts: the statement of financial performance (formerly called the profit and loss account); the statement of financial position (formerly called the balance sheet); the cash flow statement and the notes to accounts. I find the phrases 'statement of financial performance' and 'statement of financial position' confusingly similar, so at the risk of being anachronistic, I propose in this book to stick to the old-fashioned terms 'profit and loss account' and 'balance sheet'. In this section we shall deal first with the profit and loss account.

The profit made by a company is vital to its health and even its existence. When analysts pick over a company's accounts, they spend most of their time trying to work out what the ordinary profit of the company is, stripped of extraordinary and abnormal items.

There were three key words in the last sentence. *Ordinary* operations give rise to the profit for the year and comprise those revenues and expenses normally incurred in achieving the results of the enterprise and which are carried on regularly from period to period. *Abnormal* items (in current jargon, unusual items) are those items of revenue and expense which, although attributable to ordinary operations, are abnormal because of their size and

16 THE NUMBERS GAME

effect on a particular year's profit. *Extraordinary* items are outside the ordinary operations of a company and are not of a recurring nature, such as the sale of a significant business segment.[1]

Alas, these useful distinctions became blurred by the AASB in 2001. The definition of extraordinary items has been tightened to the point where they barely exist. Only some extreme event such as government appropriation or an Act of God would qualify. Abnormals used to be shown separately in the profit and loss account but now the stated profit in the P&L includes such non-recurring items as the sale of head office. Companies are required, however, to list 'unusual' items in a note to the accounts. This means a diligent investor who combs through the notes can still segregate the recurring profit items—which should be expected to contribute to profit again next year—from non-recurring items in the latest year. However, investors who want to compare the stated profit in the latest year with those of the last five or 10 years will see only the headline numbers. The only way of finding out how far the previous results were affected by abnormals/unusuals will be by getting the actual accounts from those years and poring through the notes.

Let's start with the size and quality of the company's profit. The most instructive way to do this is by using a traditional industrial company as an example. Just as an exercise, we'll go through the 1999 accounts of the old packaging and paper group (as it then was) Amcor (see Table 2.1). Amcor has since been split into halves, but its 1999 accounts remain a useful case study.

Novices gazing at a profit and loss account for the first time could be forgiven for throwing up their hands in despair and confusion. Which of these numbers is the real profit?

The short answer is that the bottom line is the real profit. For the long answer, let's go through the table line by line.

Net sales

The 1999 sales of $6048.8 million are what Amcor received for its paper and board products during that year, net of returns, discounts and allowances. Note that if they had not netted out those items, sales would have looked bigger. Companies sometimes horse around with their sales figures to make them

Table 2.1 Amcor's profit, 1998–99

Year to 30 June	1999 $m	1998 $m
Net sales	6 048.8	6 056.1
Other revenue	655.2	323.4
	6 704.0	6 379.5
Operating profit before depreciation, amortisation, interest, abnormal items and tax	811.8	767.1
Depreciation and amortisation	(252.0)	(256.4)
Operating profit before interest, abnormal items and tax	559.8	510.7
Net interest	(109.9)	(112.4)
Operating profit before abnormal items and tax	449.9	398.3
Net abnormal items	(15.9)	(291.6)
Operating profit before tax	434.0	106.7
Tax	(143.9)	(51.1)
Operating profit after tax	290.1	55.6
Outside equity interests	(6.2)	(5.1)
Net profit attributable to Amcor shareholders	283.9	50.5

look larger than they really are. In the 1980s Elders' sales figures used to include the total value of goods it sold at auction, on the grounds that it was *del credere* agent for the goods until the buyer paid. This is equivalent to a real estate agent selling a $500 000 house on which the agent will earn $15 000 commission and saying his revenue is $500 000 because the agent was at risk in the interim period between the auction and settlement. In the 1980s Elders were the biggest stock and station agents in Australia and the practice inflated their sales figures to the point where they were the largest company in Australia measured by revenue in some years.

Other revenue

This represents income derived from non-core activities. Some interest and dividends were received but the biggest item was

18 THE NUMBERS GAME

$570 million on the sale of group businesses and assets. This brings us to a core point about profit and loss (P&L) accounts. Nearly all the energy expended by analysts on P&L accounts is an attempt to separate one-off items from ongoing items. Profits generated from ongoing businesses (selling paper and containers) should be repeatable next year. These are the profits that will generate future dividends and growth. But profits generated from the sale of a business, by definition, are only going to happen once. They must be stripped out to get a clear picture of the group's profitability. The only exception is when the core business of the group is trading in capital assets, which would be a fair description of such 1980s wheeler-dealer groups as Bond Corporation and Industrial Equity. Then you might as well lump everything in together.

Operating costs

This is a line that doesn't appear, although perhaps it should. It is obtained by subtracting the operating profit of $811.8 million from the total revenue of $6704.0 million. This gives us apparent operating costs of $5892.2 million for 1999, up 5 per cent from $5612.4 million in the previous year. So despite the fact that Amcor said it had indulged in an extensive cost-cutting and rationalisation program in 1998, costs still rose slightly.

Operating profit before depreciation, amortisation, interest, abnormal items and tax

A dreadful mouthful, but this is the operating result of the business: the amount of profit actually generated before various adjustments. If you were buying a business this is the line upon which you would concentrate. Depreciation and amortisation (D&A) are non-cash items, interest depends on the level of debt and tax may depend upon your financial structure. The only adjustment you would make would be to strip out the abnormal items on the grounds they are non-repeating. That would reduce the operating profit to $795.9 million in 1999 and $475.5 million in 1998, when Amcor suffered severe abnormals because of a major restructuring. With the abnormals stripped out, we have Amcor's earnings before interest, tax, depreciation and amortisation, called EBITDA. Try to remember that acronym, because it is frequently used by analysts. The operating margin of the business is EBITDA expressed as a percentage of net sales (not total sales because that includes distorting figures in other revenue). That calculation would give Amcor an operating margin of 13.2 per cent in 1999 compared to 7.9 per cent in 1998. The 1999 figure, after the restructuring and associated costs, should be the more accurate reflection of Amcor's earning capacity.

Depreciation and amortisation

Better known as D&A. If Amcor buys a computer for $1 million which it estimates will have a five-year life, the computer will be depreciated at $200 000 a year as a charge against profit. If the computer actually lasts for ten years, then Amcor will have been underestimating its profits because it should only have been charging $100 000 a year. If the computer only lasts four years, Amcor will have overstated profits because the annual charge should have been $250 000. These examples show straight-line depreciation, which Amcor uses. Some companies charge depreciation on a reducing value basis which means that in the first year the charge would be 20 per cent of $1 million but in the second it would be 20 per cent of $800 000, bringing depreciation down to $160 000 instead of $200 000. In the third year depreciation would then be 20 per cent of $640 000, which is $128 000, and so on. Depreciation figures are necessarily arbitrary because we don't really know the working life of any asset until it's over. The best way to assess depreciation is on a comparative basis. If two companies have essentially the same equipment and one is depreciating faster than the other its bottom line will be hurting accordingly, but the conservative view of asset life may be the more realistic. As Amcor has no publicly listed competitors in Australia, the best we can do is compare the 1999 depreciation with 1998. It seems to be in the ballpark. Note that depreciation is not money actually spent during the year. It is money that will have to be spent in future to replace an asset. This assumes that the company is going to stay in the

20 THE NUMBERS GAME

same business. If BHP doesn't intend to keep making steel, argu-
ably it doesn't have to provide for the replacement of its blast
furnaces. But if it's going to sell its steel division, the steel assets
should be in the books at somewhere around market price, which
argues that they should be depreciated to market levels.

Operating profit before interest, abnormal items and tax

This was $559.8 million in 1999. If we strip out the abnormals
at this level the figure comes down to $543.9 million. That is
Amcor's earnings before interest and tax, called EBIT by analysts: another acronym worth remembering.

Net interest

The $109.9 million net interest is the difference between
$127.2 million interest stated as paid by Amcor during the year
and $17.3 million which it received. Another $28.5 million paid
in interest was capitalised.

Capitalisation of interest works like this. Let's say Amcor
had built a paper mill which had been partly funded by debt.
The construction cost of the mill was $500 million, but interest
on the debt had added another $28.5 million to that number.
Amcor has two choices. One is to charge the interest directly
against profit, which would increase the interest bill for 1999
to $138.5 million and reduce pre-tax profit by $28.5 million.
Or it can claim the interest was an integral part of the mill
and capitalise it. In that case there is no charge against profit
and the mill is shown in the balance sheet as a $528.5 million
asset instead of a $500 million asset. Capitalisation of the
$28.5 million appears to have boosted Amcor's bottom line by
roughly $9.5 million in 1999, working on its overall tax rate of
33 per cent. A conscientious analyst might make that adjustment
to the profit, but in practical terms $9.5 million is not a major
item in a net profit of $283.9 million. Capitalisation of interest
is far more important in property and construction companies,
where interest may be an important component of their costs.
Whether the capitalised interest will be recaptured in the final

sale of the asset will depend on the asset and the market. In the property bust of 1990–92, a lot of capitalised interest was written off.

If you take the pre-tax profit of $434 million and add back the interest of $101.9 million, the sum is $535.9 million. If $101.9 million is divided into that figure, we get the interest cover which is 5.26 times. In other words there is $5.26 in profits for every $1 paid in interest. That's quite a comfortable ratio. Even if interest rates were to double, Amcor would be handling its debt exposure easily. The rough rule of thumb for an ordinary industrial company such as Amcor is that debt is reaching dangerous levels when the ratio sinks below 2:1. For other types of companies, the ratio varies. Banks and financial institutions can tolerate considerably lower interest cover. Mining companies should have very high interest cover, if they pay interest at all.

Operating profit before abnormals and tax

In Amcor's case the abnormals are small enough to be ignored, but this line is always worth watching. A company which has suffered big write-offs during the year might quote this line as its profit figure. It's not.

Abnormals (unusuals)

The $15.9 million loss on abnormals is a net figure. Amcor had redundancy costs of $18.9 million and Y2K compliance costs of $6.9 million offset by profits on disposals of businesses amounting to $9.9 million (which means it didn't make much profit on that $570 million of businesses it sold). Amcor's 1999 figures look legit and are comfortingly small. In the previous year it took big hits from plant closures and rationalisation costs. The notes in the back of a company's accounts will contain one explaining the abnormals. When companies go belly-up, this is where you find the clues. It can get pretty grisly.

Operating profit before tax

Usually called profit before tax (PBT).

22 THE NUMBERS GAME

Tax

Amcor's 1999 tax of $143.9 million represents a 33 per cent rate, only a little below the prevailing 36 per cent Australian corporate rate. If a company is paying tax at a substantially higher or lower rate, it is worth examining the notes to try to work out why. A company paying more tax than it should is probably badly structured. A company paying very low rates of tax may be relying on artificial structures to minimise tax. If those structures are extinguished (by a change of law or a court ruling) and the company has to pay tax at the normal rates, its profits will diminish correspondingly. In the absence of evidence to the contrary, it should be assumed that any Australian company paying ultra-low tax is involved in litigation with the Australian Taxation Office.

Operating profit after tax

Usually called net profit after tax (NPAT). In the absence of minority interests, this is the profit number that analysts quote.

Outside equity interests

Often called minority interests. The profit in the previous line of $290.1 million is for the consolidated Amcor group, which would include everything in which it owned more than 50 per cent. However, Amcor did not own 100 per cent in some of the companies that have been consolidated. It held only 55 per cent of PT Indopack Pratama in Indonesia, for example. The holders of the rest of the equity in such companies are entitled to their share of the profits there. If such companies make losses, then the minority holders take their share of those too.

Net profit attributable to Amcor shareholders

Finally, the bottom line. This is Amcor's real profit for 1999, although we could deduct $9.5 million for the after-tax effect of the capitalised interest. But for the sake of the exercise, let's stick to Amcor's quoted profit figure of $283.9 million. That's a 462 per cent increase on the 1998 profit, but comparisons are pretty meaningless considering the reconstruction hit Amcor took in 1998. If we look back over a few years, it is apparent that Amcor's rationalisation was yielding fewer sales (see Table 2.2). The rationalisation cost it heavily in 1997 and 1998. Profit bounced back in 1999, but a comparison of profit to sales ratios shows Amcor was still not enjoying the profitability of 1995 and 1996. Although if we really knew the inside story, perhaps those years should have been attributed with some of the losses that were finally chalked up in 1997 and 1998.

Table 2.2 Amcor over six years

	1999 $m	1998 $m	1997 $m	1996 $m	1995 $m
Net sales	6 048.8	6 056.1	6 149.8	6 423.8	6 595.7
Profit	283.9	50.5	(80.1)	338.8	359.7
Profit/sales	4.7%	0.8%	(1.3%)	5.3%	5.5%

Return on shareholders' funds

Now that we have the profit, we can do a few more numbers. Shareholders' funds of Amcor as at 30 June 1999 totalled $2679.5 million. The $283.9 million profit represents a return of 10.6 per cent.

Earnings per share

More meaningful is earnings per share (EPS). Amcor had 638.1 million fully paid shares on issue as at 30 June, which meant the $283.9 million represents EPS of 44.5 cents per share on year-end capital. (Issued capital fell a bit during the year because of a share buyback.)

Price/earnings ratio

Also known as the P/E ratio or P/E multiple. This is the share price divided by the EPS. When the annual report was issued in 1999 Amcor's share price was around $7. That meant its P/E ratio was 700 divided by 44.5, which was 15.7 times. P/E ratios get a lot of attention from analysts. What the P/E ratio really measures is the degree of heat in the market and in particular stocks. During market slumps, P/E ratios can fall to 12 or 10 or even single digits. Broadly, any stock selling on a P/E below 12 is in bargain territory and worth serious consideration as a buying proposition provided that its E (earnings) is sustainable. When P/E ratios go above 20, they have historically been regarded as high.

P/E ratios should also be regarded in conjunction with interest rates. When interest rates are low, and dividend yields are correspondingly low, simple arithmetic tells us that P/E ratios will tend to be higher.

When comparing similar industrials, it is always worthwhile comparing their P/E ratios. If one bank is on a P/E of 10, while another is on a P/E of 12, then the logical buy is the bank on 10 provided all other things are equal (which they never are).

Finally, note that P/E ratios can only be applied to companies which have E. In the late 1990s the Australian share market was hit by a wave of technology stocks that were sometimes highly priced without having any E at all. We will deal with these a bit later. Meanwhile the best advice is that unless you know what you're doing, stick with stocks that have P/Es.

Payout ratio

In 1999 Amcor paid $249.3 million in dividends. That is a payout ratio of 87.8 per cent of our $283.9 million profit. Alternatively, dividend cover (the number of times dividend was covered by profit) was 1.14 times. This is a pretty skinny dividend cover or a very high payout ratio, depending on which way you want to phrase it. The rule of thumb used to be that a company should pay about half its profits in dividends and plough the rest back into expansion. The fashion in the 1990s was to lift this payout ratio towards 60 or 70 per cent, but even by that standard Amcor's 1999 payout ratio was exceedingly high. If it didn't show evidence that profit was rising—and fairly soon—the market would start marking the shares down.

The point about high payout ratios is that they leave no room for increasing dividends in the future unless there is a dramatic rise in profitability. In 1999 Amcor's dividends per share (DPS) was 39 cents. At the then share price of $7, the dividend yield was 5.5 per cent. That was a good yield for a blue chip such as Amcor at the time, but the possibility of growth in the following year was small. High payout ratios can be ameliorated if the company has a dividend reinvestment plan (DRIP) scheme. If a proportion of shareholders opt to take their dividends in scrip rather than cash, then the cash payout is correspondingly reduced. Amcor didn't have a DRIP scheme in 1999.

The balance sheet (now called the statement of financial performance)

A balance sheet is a snapshot in time of a company's state of affairs. Specifically, it is a snapshot taken at the close of trading on its balance date, which in Australia is usually 30 June.

It's called a balance sheet because it's supposed to balance. A company's assets total exactly the same figure as its liabilities to creditors plus its liabilities to shareholders.

Sticking with good old Amcor, let's look at its balance sheet in 1999 (Table 2.3).

This formidable table of numbers can be intimidating, but let's pick our way through it by first concentrating on the main ones. In 1999 Amcor had total assets of $6353.2 million. If they could be sold for that amount by a liquidator, he or she would then have to pay off all the company's liabilities, which total $3629.5 million. Our hypothetical liquidator would then have $2723.7 million left over, which could be distributed among the shareholders. That's why that figure is called *shareholders' funds*.

The $2723.7 million is also called *net assets* (that is, total assets net of liabilities). If we divide that figure by the 638.1 million shares Amcor had on issue we get a net asset backing (NAB) of $4.26 per share.[2]

26 THE NUMBERS GAME

Table 2.3 Amcor's balance sheet, 1998–99

Year ending 30 June	1999 $m	1998 $m
Current assets		
Cash	188.6	264.2
Receivables	905.9	1 038.3
Inventories	882.0	967.0
Total current assets	1 976.5	2 269.5
Non-current assets		
Receivables	98.8	103.2
Investments	200.1	279.0
Property, plant and equipment	3 503.0	3 820.7
Intangibles	407.1	510.9
Other	167.7	196.9
Total non-current assets	4 376.7	4 910.7
Total assets	**6 353.2**	**7 180.2**
Current liabilities		
Accounts payable	706.5	838.2
Borrowings	392.4	485.9
Provisions	411.8	448.2
Total current liabilities	1 510.7	1 772.3
Non-current liabilities		
Accounts payable	7.6	10.4
Borrowings	1 191.4	1 588.9
Provisions	493.6	493.4
Total non-current liabilities	1 692.6	2 092.7
Undated subordinated convertible securities	426.2	426.2
Total liabilities	**3 629.5**	**4 291.2**
Shareholders' equity		
Share capital	1 856.3	641.9
Reserves	410.3	1 813.4
Retained profits	412.9	386.4
Shareholders' equity attributable to Amcor members	2 679.5	2 841.7
Outside equity interests	44.2	47.3
Net assets	**2 723.7**	**2 889.0**

Gearing

One important indicator of a company's health is the balance between external liabilities and shareholders' funds. To put it another way, the degree to which a company is funded by its creditors as opposed to its shareholders. Debt finance is a two-edged sword. If the company operates well, the use of debt increases the return to owners. But if the company is run badly—or circumstances turn adverse—it can put the company at risk.

Gearing is found by expressing external liabilities ($3629.5 million in this case) as a percentage of total assets ($6353.2 million). The calculation comes out to 57.1 per cent. In analysts' shorthand, Amcor was 57 per cent geared. This can also be expressed as a ratio, in which case it comes out to 1.33:1 (the gearing ratio). The traditional rule of thumb is that a company should be roughly half funded by debt and half funded by equity. Amcor looks a tad high, but not enough to cause concern. Anything between 40 per cent and 60 per cent is generally considered okay. A company with higher gearing than that could be incurring debt at dangerous levels. A company with gearing under that range may not be aggressive enough.

The desirable gearing level varies between types of company. Banks and financiers can tolerate high levels of gearing. Mining companies should generally be low geared.

There are other ways of calculating gearing. Some analysts calculate it on the basis of debt to total assets. Some use net debt (total debt less cash) to total assets. Calculating gearing on these bases gives lower gearing ratios because any provisions among the liabilities are dropped out. So these methods are popular among companies who want their gearing to look lower.

PREJUDICE 4

There's an element of bogosity about any gearing calculation that drops out the provisions or uses any other arithmetic to reduce the figure you'd get by simply expressing total liabilities as a percentage of total assets.

28 THE NUMBERS GAME

The underlying assumption of the fancier gearing calculations is usually that provisions are not really liabilities. They bloody well are. In the liquidation of National Textiles, for example, provisions for employee redundancy and other items left nearly nothing for creditors. Stated provisions are for items such as accrued long service leave, holiday pay, tax and dividends. They really are liabilities of the company and should, to my mind anyway, be recognised. So whenever a company's gearing is shown on a debt or net debt basis recalculate it on the basis of total liabilities to total assets. The picture is usually less pretty, and sometimes it changes from Dorian Gray to the painting he kept in the attic. Let's plod through the balance sheet line by line.

Current assets

These comprise cash on hand plus any assets that are expected to be realised within the next twelve months. Usually this is straightforward but occasionally someone puts odd assets in here. When Christopher Skase was running Qintex the current assets blew out to more than $800 million because they included hundreds of millions in television stations and program rights on the grounds that they were all held for resale and therefore could not be considered long-term assets. It also meant, under prevailing accounting lore, that as current assets they did not have to be depreciated. That was just as well because Qintex's profitability was always razor-thin and any further depreciation would have pushed him into losses.

Cash Not necessarily held in the safe, as it can also be in liquid form such as trading accounts. Where a company has no income, it is vital to compare its cash holdings with the rate of spending. (See Chapter 3.)

Receivables Money owing by customers, whom we presume are going to pay.

Inventories Raw material, stores, work in progress (which in this case would be items such as pulp going through the mill) and finished goods awaiting resale. Note that Amcor's inventories have fallen $85 million from the previous year, when they looked rather high.

There is no golden rule as to what comprises the 'right' level of inventory. The best you can do is to compare the level with previous years. A company which is holding too much inventory is having problems moving its products. One calculation which is sometimes useful is the stock-turn ratio. Amcor's notes to accounts showed that finished goods accounted for $453 million as at 30 June 1999 and $462.2 million the previous year. The average of these two figures is $457.6 million. If we divide that average figure into the sales for the year ($6048.8 million) we find that Amcor turned over its average inventory level 13.2 times during 1998–99. If we divide 13.2 into 365 we can express that ratio alternatively as an average 27.6 day stock turn.

If you plod back through previous balance sheets you can calculate the stock-turn ratio for prior years and work out whether a company is turning over its stock more quickly or more slowly. The problem with this calculation is that a devious-minded company can play the numbers game by repainting its year-end stock figures. A manufacturer, for example, can consign truckloads of goods to retailers on 30 June. Hey presto, dead stock laying around the warehouse has magically been transformed into receivables from the retailers. If the retailers send the trucks back on 1 July, a purblind auditor (yes, there are a few) might still rubber-stamp them as receivables. Sometimes the manufacturer is able to persuade friendly retailers to keep the stock until the auditor has signed the accounts. The persuasion is a lot easier if the retailer's balance date differs from the manufacturer's, because otherwise the retailer will be shown holding too much stock. Meanwhile the manufacturer's stock levels are down and its stock-turn ratio looks terrific.

If games like this are being played, no analyst has a prayer of discovering them from the balance sheet. The game will only be detectable by someone well plugged into the retailers' gossip circle.

Non-current assets

Also called fixed assets. These assets represent everything the company doesn't intend to sell this year. These are the assets

30 THE NUMBERS GAME

which produce the company's wealth, which in Amcor's case include head office, paper mills, forests and investments.

Receivables Normally receivables, by definition, are a short-term asset but Amcor has a few cheques due to come in over longer periods—mostly loans to associated companies but also a few loans to directors and employees.

Investments Sometimes investments are shown as a separate category from other long-term assets. It depends whether they are portfolio investments which can be easily sold or whether they are strategic investments that are important to the company's business. By law the company has to show the market value of investments as well as the book value. In Amcor's case roughly half the investments were listed. Notes to the accounts showed they had a market value $20 million above book value, so we should be able to assume that the total figure for investments is reasonably conservative.

Notes to accounts relating to investments should always be checked, because real horrors can be lurking there. Loans to associated companies may be entered in at their original amount plus capitalised interest, even though there is no hope of full—or sometimes any—recovery. The market value of listed investments should be checked against the book value. Where the investments are shares in related or interlocking companies it pays to be a little suspicious—particularly where small companies have relatively large investments in each other.

For example, if Company A holds a substantial investment in Company B, what happened to Company B's share price at balance date? Did some mysteriously enthusiastic buyer shove the price up from 8 cents to 10 cents, which is easy enough to do in an illiquid stock when nobody is watching? If they did, that represents a 25 per cent increase in the value of Company A's holding. If the price of Company B has fallen back again since balance date it is an almost certain sign that someone was playing games on 30 June.

Property, plant and equipment Property, plant and equipment (PPE) usually speaks for itself in manufacturing companies.

Check that these assets are being depreciated at a reasonable rate and there have not been any unrealistic revaluations in the latest year. This asset is usually most questionable when held in property companies. The fact that the company has spent X amount of money developing a property does not necessarily mean that the property can be sold for that much.

Intangibles Welcome to the most disputed area in corporate accounting. Assets have traditionally been divided into two types. The first are tangibles, such as factories, office blocks and paper clips. The second are intangibles, which can be further divided into brand names and goodwill. Brand names and mastheads such as Coca-Cola, Vegemite and *The Australian Women's Weekly* obviously have some value to their owners. Goodwill is more arcane.

Let's say Company A takes over Company B for $50 million, but Company B has only $30 million in tangible assets. Those $30 million of assets will go onto Company A's balance sheet at book value, but how do we account for the remaining $20 million? The answer is to call it goodwill. Goodwill is not paid out of sheer Dickensian bonhomie, but should represent some advantage to Company A. It may be that the takeover of Company B gives Company A the chance to acquire a larger share of a particular market or access to a valuable distribution network. It may be that Company A can sink some of Company B's troublesome competitive products. It may be that the takeover means Company A will acquire an excellent management team. There are heaps of reasons for paying a premium to take over a company and sometimes they're justified.

How these intangible assets—brand names and goodwill—should be measured, justified and depreciated has exercised a great deal of accounting intellect in Australia over the past decade. The problem has also resulted in some arcane accounting standards and some bizarre numbers appearing in company reports.

My heretical advice is to ignore the accounting standards and look at the bottom line. If an asset is producing earnings of $1 million a year and the prevailing price/earnings ratio is 20, then it can be assumed to be worth $20 million. That test does not differentiate between tangible and intangible assets. As far as I'm concerned, the only difference between a brand name and a factory is that the real estate on which the factory is built will have some residual value, and maybe the building as well. Otherwise, assets are worth what they can earn. And if they're not generating earnings now, they had better start generating them damned soon or be written down to zero. This bloody-minded attitude is worth keeping in mind whenever there is a rage in the stock market for some new wave of companies that are poorly understood and not yet producing earnings, such as nickel stocks in 1970 and hi-tech stocks in 2000. The average investor cannot hope to evaluate state-of-the-art (or alleged state-of-the-art) advances in computer software, telephony and biotechnology. But it's easy enough to see whether the great scientific breakthrough the promoters are selling is yet generating earnings, or at least sales. Here endeth the lesson on intangibles.

PREJUDICE 5

If it doesn't earn profits this year and won't next year, it isn't an asset, whether tangible or intangible.

Other assets The $167.7 million includes $144.9 million in future tax benefits. A generation of Australian accountants has accepted a future tax benefit as a genuine asset, but I still have mutinous doubts.

The logic of future tax benefits runs like this. If a company makes a profit of $1 million and the prevailing tax rate is 30 per cent, then it will pay $300 000 tax and its net profit will come down to $700 000. So far, so good. However, if a company makes a loss of $1 million, it will not only pay no tax, but the loss can be carried forward to be deductible against future profits. So if next year our company makes a profit of $1 million or more, it can deduct the $1 million loss and its tax will accordingly be reduced in that year by $300 000. So when it incurred the $1 million loss it also generated a future tax benefit of $300 000.

Note that this tax benefit will only be realised if (a) the company makes a profit in future; (b) the tax rate stays the same; and (c) the tax law stays the same. Broadly, the Australian tax law will allow the loss to be deductible if the company is still pursuing the same activity. If Amcor's losses were incurred in paper-making it can deduct them from future profits made from paper-making, but not from profits from other activities. Tax losses can have a value. Companies containing tax losses are routinely sold to investors who can use them. If the losses relate to investments, then just about anybody could use them. But if they relate to paper-making, the number of buyers would be limited.

The future tax benefits account for all but $22.8 million of Amcor's 'other assets'. The rest were unidentified and in Amcor are relatively insignificant, so investors need not worry about them. But many a nasty little monster has lurked in this category of 'other' assets, which is where all sorts of capitalised expenses go to hide.

The 1989 Bond Corporation accounts contained nearly $400 million in 'other assets'. Upon inspection, $280 million of that turned out to be deferred capitalised expenses, mostly related to advertising and marketing. These are deeply dubious assets, particularly in Bond's case. The logic is that if Bond spent money advertising, say, Swan beer, the money the company spent was building the brand name and making Swan a more valuable asset. So instead of being expensed against the profit and loss account, the cash spent on advertising could instead be capitalised and labelled as an asset. In fact, Swan was actually losing market share to Carlton & United at the time despite an orgy of advertising by Bond. The capitalisation of expenses was unjustifiable. When looking at assets of this nature, it's always worth asking two questions: 'How much could this be sold for?' and 'Who would buy it?' If the answers are zero and nobody, well, you have your answers.

PREJUDICE 6

If a company capitalises enough of its expenses it can declare a terrific profit accompanied by a strong balance sheet and only one problem: it's broke.

Current liabilities

This term covers all liabilities existing at balance date which will fall due within twelve months.

34 THE NUMBERS GAME

Accounts payable The first item on the liabilities side is the amounts which Amcor owes to trade creditors, generally people who have supplied it with goods and services and had accounts outstanding at the balance date. Amcor owes its suppliers $706.5 million. Note that back in current assets, Amcor was owed $905.9 million by its customers. That's a nice, comfortable ratio. Amcor's owed a bit more money by trade debtors than it owed to trade creditors.

Borrowings Any borrowings that are repayable within the coming twelve months should be included here. The bank overdraft will come in here ($22 million for Amcor at balance date), accompanied by bank bills and any long-term debt which is nearing maturity.

Provisions Amounts set aside for such expenses as tax, dividends and employee entitlements (holiday pay, long-service leave, etc.).

Total current liabilities

It's always nice if current liabilities are smaller than current assets. As Amcor has current assets totalling $1976.5 million and current liabilities of $1510.7, the current ratio is 1.3 times. As more money is due to come in the front door over the next twelve months than is due to flow out the back, Amcor should be under no pressure to find any funding accommodation in the short term.

Modern analysts are fairly relaxed about the current ratio. An adverse current ratio can be tolerated in a company with strong cash flow. However, when times get tight and cash flow dries, this ratio can be an indicator of the company's likely future health.

Non-current liabilities

All liabilities which fall due more than twelve months from balance date. There is a tendency among analysts to look only at the debt component, but it should not be forgotten that the accounts payable and provisions are also liabilities and will have to be paid somehow.

Undated subordinated convertible securities

Quite a mouthful, but let's deal with it one word at a time. Amcor issued two series of unsecured notes. One set was due to mature in 2006 and one in 2003. But they are redeemable only at Amcor's option, so for practical purposes they are undated. They may never have to be redeemed and hence may never mature.

They are subordinated to all other obligations of the company apart from share capital. In a liquidation, holders of these notes would stand in the queue behind all other secured and unsecured creditors. Only the shareholders would rank behind them.

The notes are convertible into Amcor shares. One series is convertible at $9.35 and the others at a variable rate which in late 1999 was nearly $10. The rule of thumb is that any convertible security should be regarded as debt as long as it is out of the money (that is, the conversion price is higher than the prevailing market price). If the share price rises to the point where it pays to convert, then it can be fairly reclassified as equity.

Net assets

Skipping a few lines we get to the bottom of the balance sheet, where total shareholders' equity is shown as $2723.7 million. This is the amount we get if total liabilities of $3629.5 million are subtracted from total assets of $6353.2 million.

Outside equity interests

Amcor shareholders don't own the whole of the net assets. That is because these are consolidated accounts, which show 100 per cent of the assets and liabilities of the companies in the group which are controlled by Amcor. But Amcor does not own 100 per cent of all of them. There are minority shareholders,

36 THE NUMBERS GAME

particularly in some overseas companies. Where these companies have an excess of assets over liabilities, the minority shareholders are entitled to their stakes, which total $44 million. By deducting that figure from net assets of $2723.7 million we get the net assets attributable to Amcor shareholders, which is $2679.5 million. If this figure is divided by the 638 million shares on issue we get a net asset backing (NAB) per share of $4.20.

When the share price of a company falls below NAB, then either the company is undergoing tough times or is being poorly run, or both. In those circumstances it is usually not long before a corporate raider arrives on the scene. If a company's NAB figure is accurate and it can be taken over for substantially less, then breaking it up should be a paying proposition. Fortunes have been made on that tactic.

Referring again to the 1989 accounts of Bond Corporation (which were a collector's item), net assets of the group were shown as $1.8 billion, but minority interests totalled $1.9 billion. In other words, the only bits of Bond Corporation which retained any value were those owned by minority shareholders. When the minorities were netted out, the rest of Bond Corporation had a deficiency of $116 million. No wonder it collapsed.

The cash flow statement

One of the biggest advances in corporate disclosure in recent years has been the advent of the cash flow statement. Profit is an accounting concept. It is the result of a number of assumptions about collectability of bad debts, depreciation rates, value of investments, business write-downs and so forth. Cash, by comparison, is what actually flowed in and out of the company during the year.

Cash flows come in three categories:

1 operating (the actual cash moving in and out of the business as it provides goods or services);
2 investing (relating to the acquisition or disposal of any

non-current asset, such as property, plant or long-term investments); and

3 financing (anything relating to the financial structure, such as issues or buybacks of shares and raising or repayment of borrowings).

Table 2.4 shows Amcor's cash flow statement for 1999.

Table 2.4 is fairly self-explanatory. All figures in brackets are cash outflows, the rest are cash inflows. We'll now go through the main sections of the cash flow statement.

Operating activities

Cash flows of Amcor's business. The operating margin (the difference between receipts from customers and payments to suppliers and employees) is a healthy $746.4 million. After allowing for dividend flows, tax and interest, the actual operating cash flow of the business was $629.6 million. This operating surplus represents a return of just over 10 per cent on sales revenue. That's a nice margin.

Note that this operating surplus of $629.6 million does not align with the operating profit of $811.8 million in the profit and loss account (Table 2.1). That is because of various accounting adjustments. Notes to the accounts of any public company give a reconciliation of the operating cash flow with the accounting profit.

A lay reader need not worry too much about this reconciliation as long as the numbers seem to be in the same ballpark. There is a danger signal, however, if cash flow is substantially less than stated profit. Amcor's cash flow was a bit too far below stated profit for comfort.

There have been plenty of more extreme cases, however. One was the half-year accounts of Digicall for December 1995.[3] Digicall was a reseller of mobile phone services for Vodafone and in hindsight probably hit the digital telecommunications revolution a few years too early. The prospectus, launched in the middle of 1995, forecast revenue of $21.3 million for the six months to December 1995.

In the event, Digicall's interim statement reported revenues

38 THE NUMBERS GAME

Table 2.4 Amcor's cash flow statement, year to 30 June 1999

	$m
Operating activities	
Receipts from customers	6 191.4
Payments to suppliers and employees	(5 445.0)
Dividends received	32.3
Interest received	17.5
Interest paid	(157.0)
Tax paid	(40.3)
Other income	30.7
Net cash from operating activities	**629.6**
Investing activities	
Loans to associated companies and others	(10.7)
Loans repaid by assoc. companies and others	4.4
Acquisition of businesses	(18.2)
Acquisition of property, plant and equipment	(422.9)
Sale of businesses	533.4
Sale of investments	0.2
Sale of property, plant and equipment	30.2
Net cash from investing activities	**116.4**
Financing activities	
Dividends paid	(247.9)
Share buyback	(37.2)
Share issues and calls	12.8
Loans from other persons	1.7
Loans repaid to other persons	(28.9)
Proceeds from borrowings	179.6
Repayment of borrowings	(573.9)
Principal lease repayments	(21.8)
Net cash from financing activities	**(715.6)**
Net increase in cash held	30.4
Cash at beginning of year	259.4
Exchange rate changes on translation of foreign currency cash flows	(91.6)
Cash at end of year	**198.2**

of \$31.2 million in the profit and loss account. However, heavy start-up costs and amortisation knocked the net result back to a loss of \$1.9 million before abnormals. This sort of start-up result for a high-tech company could have been tolerated by any investor who didn't read through to the cash flow statement, which looked like Table 2.5.

Table 2.5 Digicall cash flow, six months to December 1995

	\$000
Cash receipts in course of operations	8 090
Cash payments in course of operations	(3 571)
Net operational cash flow	4 519

Just a moment! We have a problem here with the top line. How can a company state in its P&L account that it has revenue of \$31.2 million when it has only received cash of \$8.1 million? Stripped of accounting jargon, the answer is that Digicall was front-ending.

Let's say a Digicall subscriber had signed a twelve-month contract in September for \$100 a month. The amount of cash Digicall would have received by Christmas was \$300. But Digicall was counting the whole \$1200 as revenue received within the period. It had been contracted to be paid but it hadn't actually been paid—a frightfully important difference. Contracts can blow up for all sorts of reasons, particularly on mobile phones. Mobile phones can be lost or stolen or the owners may leave town or even the country.

Taking revenue into account before the cash has been received, or even payable, is known as front-end loading or front-ending. It is one of the commonest ways of inflating revenue (and hence profit) in company accounts. Front-ending can happen in the accounts of any company which sells products or services on a time-payments basis—notably property and finance companies.

40 THE NUMBERS GAME

PREJUDICE 7

If a company's stated revenue in the profit and loss account is substantially higher than the cash it has received in the cash flow statement, the company can be taken to have been front-end loading until it conclusively proves otherwise.

Investing activities

Amcor, like most big companies, is constantly reinvesting in its business. It buys new companies and machinery and sells those it no longer needs. These activities generated net cash of $116.4 million.

Financing activities

Operating and investing activities together generated $746 million surplus cash. What did Amcor do with the money? Most of it (nearly $400 million net, the difference between $573.9 million and $179.6 million) was spent repaying borrowings. Another $247.9 million was spent paying dividends. The net result of financing activities was a drain of $715.6 million, or only $30.4 million less than the total cash inflow of $746 million.

Cash at end of year

The net $30 million increase in cash for the year was more than wiped out (in A$ terms) by exchange rate fluctuations. Actual cash at balance date was down $61 million to $198.2 million. Amcor actually suffered a cash drain for the year, which would not have been detected by a reader who merely relied on its profit and loss account.

So the cash flow statement tells how the operating business performed for the year, what investments the company undertook and how it paid for them. This is quite valuable information in gauging the underlying health of a company's business, as opposed to the stated profit in the profit and loss account, which may have been massaged considerably.

It should be pointed out that Amcor's share price slid nastily in 1999–2000, diving from around $7 to as low as $4.50. Part of that fall was due to some of the weaknesses pointed out in the analysis above, but there were other factors. The board decided to split Amcor's paper-making business away from its packaging business. This meant Amcor would be divided into two smaller companies and so it fell below the size of company that some fund managers would invest in. But mostly the fall was because old industrials such as Amcor had become unfashionable in an era when technology stocks were all the buzz.

That's about all a lay investor needs to know to analyse a set of accounts of an industrial company. But not all companies are industrials. Let's have a look at a few other categories.

3

Types of companies

Our previous section dealt with Amcor to give readers a picture of an archetypal industrial company. Once upon a time such companies dominated the share lists of the Australian Stock Exchange. Today, however, they have become a minority. There are several other types of companies and often they need to be analysed in different ways. The basics remain the same, but there are extra points that an analyst needs to consider.

In this chapter we will look at a few different types of company, concentrating on those that have been fashionable in recent years or which are large in the Australian market.

TMT companies

A great boom began running in Australian telcos, media and technology (TMT) stocks in 1998 which peaked in March 2000 then suffered a great shake out. The boom began on the Nasdaq Exchange in New York a year or two earlier and spread around the world. By 2001 a great many dotcoms had gone belly-up, but the boom is worth exploring for a moment because it had characteristics that are common to all booms. At any given time the market is likely to go crazy about a particular bunch of stocks and put them at prices that defy traditional valuations. In the long run, however, the traditional valuations emerge (which means the overpriced stocks come down in a real hurry). So let's spend a minute looking at the TMTs.

Traditional stock valuations (as expressed in the preceding

chapter analysing Amcor's accounts) were thrown out of the window because a 'new paradigm' had arrived. The world of TMT stocks was both converging and expanding. The convergence was occurring as the traditionally discrete industries of newspaper publishing, television broadcasting, computers and telephones all began to run into each other under new technological applications, with the Internet serving as a catalyst. Newspapers developed Internet websites that displayed the day's news and advertisements, as well as offering other services. Technology made it possible for television to be broadcast over the Internet and even onto mobile phones. Australia's biggest pay television network, Foxtel, was owned by a phone company (Telstra), and two media companies, Publishing & Broadcasting Limited (PBL) and News Corp. PBL's main media interests in Australia were in television while News Corp's main interest in Australia was newspapers. The main barriers to convergence were legislative (such as Australia's prohibitions on cross-ownership of newspapers and television).

The expansion was occurring as the players tried to get bigger in Australia and expand overseas. Telstra took strategic stakes in Sausage Software, Solution 6 and Computershare. John Fairfax, the most traditional of Australian newspaper publishers, tried to buy an indirect stake in Ozemail, an Internet service provider. Hundreds of start-up companies floated with ambitious plans to carve themselves a niche in the new global markets. Voxson, for example, was floated in Brisbane with the aim of getting a foothold as a worldwide mobile phone manufacturer.

Share prices for TMT stocks went seriously bananas in the wildest share market boom in Australia's history. There were several reasons for public enthusiasm.

1   Since the Keating recession of 1990–92 there had been a slow return to prosperity. By the end of the 1990s, Australians were ready to start a bout of speculation.
2   Over the same decade of the 1990s interest rates had fallen to their lowest levels since the 1960s. As always, this tended to flush investors out of the fixed interest market into equities.
3   Direct public ownership of shares greatly increased in Australia during the 1990s owing to the privatisation of the

44 THE NUMBERS GAME

Commonwealth Bank, Qantas, GIO and several other enterprises previously owned by governments, including most notably the partial privatisation of Telstra. All these floats listed at handsome premiums, giving their holders a warm glow about the stock market. In addition many policyholders in insurance companies became shareholders as those institutions demutualised, including the largest insurance companies in the nation: AMP, Colonial and National Mutual. The holders of these shares got them as gifts and did very handsomely indeed. Their glow about the market was even warmer. Some of these new shareholders spread their wings and started speculating in technology stocks.

4   Australia was watching the exciting birth of a totally new global industry. Many local companies were claiming they were going to be a part of the worldwide Net-based new era.

For all these reasons, Australians plunged enthusiastically into TMT stocks. Market capitalisations soared into the stratosphere.

Before getting cynical about the tech boom, it should be remembered that it was inspired by some genuinely fantastic success stories. Cisco Systems in the USA was started in a garage by a married couple and grew to be the world's largest company. A lot of American businesses went from start-ups to US$200 to US$300 million revenue. That's extraordinary. But excited punters drove stock prices out of control.

By the March quarter of 2000, Microsoft was raking in revenue at the rate of US$43 billion a year and its net income was running around US$10 billion. At that time it had a market capitalisation of US$350 billion, putting it on 35 times earnings —a high multiple even given Microsoft's undeniable success. A few months earlier, Microsoft had been capitalised at US$550 billion, or 55 times earnings. Oracle had a market capitalisation of US$220 billion when its core business was probably worth US$60 billion tops, which meant its share price contained some US$160 billion blue sky. Ariba Inc and Commerce One Inc were vying to be the leaders in marketplace exchange technology. Their combined capitalisation was US$70 billion, but the market they were fighting for was worth only about US$5 billion. It didn't necessarily matter if a tech stock didn't have earnings. If it was carving a niche in a market where it would enjoy 20 per cent or so share in two or three years' time and maintain a 20 per cent margin, it could be priced accordingly. But to justify the capitalisation, a tech stock had to have invented something new, because the markets in existing technology had become crowded very quickly and there was no room for new players. In this scramble for market share, Australian stocks were at an inherent disadvantage compared to US stocks, although there were some promising Aussies around.

One stock which epitomised the boom in Australia was ecorp, a spin-off of PBL. Ecorp comprised the Ticketek ticket-selling business, an online broking firm and an online auction firm. Punters were fired with enormous optimism for this group, partly because PBL (and hence the near-magic name of Kerry Packer) held 80 per cent of the stock. The shares were issued at $1.20 in mid-1999 and raced to $8.60 at their height in early 2000. As there were 670 million shares on issue, that price capitalised ecorp at $5.7 billion. This seemed a little high for a company whose last interim report showed revenue running at an annualised rate of $55 million. Ecorp was trading on 100 times revenue. Not profit, revenue. Ecorp wasn't yet making profits. A fairly enthusiastic Goldman Sachs analysis of the company had forecast that it would enjoy EBITDA of $1 million in 2002. At its peak, therefore, it was trading at 5700 times EBITDA in two years hence.

In 2003, Packer bought back the minority shares for 55c. It was less than half the value at which they had been floated, but more than ecorp's business was worth by then.

However, ecorp did illustrate the share market's abandonment of the price/earnings ratio as a yardstick. The P/E multiple had historically been quoted as the ratio of the prevailing share price to the earnings per share—and by earnings it meant net profit after tax (NPAT).

The bulk of the stocks in the technology boom didn't have earnings and it had to be doubted whether some of them ever would have earnings. So in place of the traditional P/E multiple, new multiples began to appear. Companies began talking about their prospective P/EBIT multiple or their prospective P/EBITDA multiple. ChaosMusic showed innovation by postulating a

46   THE NUMBERS GAME

P/EBITDAM multiple. That stood for price as a multiple of earnings before interest, tax, depreciation, amortisation and marketing costs. Administration costs were about the only significant item they hadn't stripped out. Some companies went straight to a price/revenue multiple.

All these new multiples ignored one historic fact. Until you have earnings you can't pay dividends and ultimately dividends, or the prospect of them, are the prime reason for holding a piece of paper.

Let's go back to basics for a second. Anyone who has some money has several choices. They can buy a house or a car or a holiday or food, for example. Why forgo these material pleasures in favour of investing, where all they will have is a humdrum piece of paper to look at? The answer is because they expect to make more money.

There are two ways to make money out of a piece of paper. One is when it produces capital gains. The piece of paper rises in value and they sell it. The second is when the piece of paper produces an income stream, either in the form of dividends or interest. Very few of the pieces of paper issued by start-up technology companies in 1999–2000 were likely to pay dividends in the foreseeable future. Most of the punters who bought them were hoping for a quick capital gain. But the trouble with capital gains is that they cannot go on for infinity. Sooner or later all stocks hit their maximum price and then turn around and start going down again. In early 2000 this even happened to the US giant Microsoft after it lost the Netscape case.

Okay, the proposition needs some qualifications. A start-up Internet stock may not make money for several years because it is investing in getting market share, aiming to become a monopolist or oligopolist of its share of the Internet or telephony or whatever. After it has become an established monopolist, or oligopolist, it will be in a position to squeeze huge profits out of its position. It will be an enormously valuable company.

PREJUDICE 8

I have an overwhelming preference for companies where the dividends are in the foreseeable future, not the unforeseeable.

As the early results from the first year or so of the start-up companies of 1998 and 1999 started rolling in to the Australian Stock Exchange (ASX), it was notable that several of them were not achieving prospectus forecasts. Why not?

Some had struck heavy competition. Some had planned projects which cost more to build than had been budgeted and taken longer to complete. Customers had fallen short of budget. Costs of servicing clients—particularly for any company engaged in the brave new world of e-commerce—had been higher than expected.

Does anything strike readers about these reasons? Yes, that's right—they're exactly the same reasons that companies in old-fashioned industries give for not meeting prospectus targets.

PREJUDICE 9

When a new company starts a new venture in a new industry it is not only likely, but almost certain, to hit obstacles that it has not foreseen. It would be little short of miraculous if it didn't.

The Net industries may have been new but they were becoming cartelised quickly. In 1999, the USA saw 35 companies floated to engage in electronic B2C (business-to-consumer) operations. By early 2000, 26 of those companies had suffered share price crashes of 80 per cent to 90 per cent. The reason was that the B2C industry had already become cartelised, with 75 per cent of B2C being done on five websites.[1]

The newly launched companies of the Net boom had not discovered some 'philosopher's stone' whereby they could suddenly make billions as if by magic (although some of their vendors did very well). The old-fashioned rules of business still applied—creditors had to be paid, getting projects off the ground took hard work, and stiff competition shredded prices and added to costs.

Sorting through the maelstrom of tech companies, it seemed impossible that a high proportion of them would establish businesses as viable as their prospectuses forecast (apart from anything else, many of them were in competition with each other). However, it seemed probable that several of them would succeed.

48 THE NUMBERS GAME

The prime requisites for a start-up technology company's success were a unique asset and the managerial skill to develop it. Unfortunately, there has never been any way of discerning these two critical elements by reading a start-up company's accounts— except in hindsight. But there are a couple of important factors that can be read in the accounts.

One item which should be accurately stated in the accounts is the cash on hand at balance date. It is useful to compare this to net expenditure in the past year and estimate how long the cash is likely to last. The longer a company can keep going, the better its chances of success. Nearly all the Australian technology boom stocks had raised substantial amounts of cash and by early 2000 had at least a year's cash on hand.

A frequent flaw in technology company budgets is that they are concerned only with the development of the product or service. Inventors, particularly, seem to be under the impression that they only have to announce the invention of a better mousetrap and the world will flock to their doorstep. The truth in the modern world is that any new product requires a great deal of marketing. The fact that it is a superior product may not mean it succeeds when attacking a market already dominated by an entrenched competitor, as Beta found when it took on VHS in video cassettes.

PREJUDICE 10

Inventors seem to think that the only cost they have to worry about is development of the product. They believe that marketing costs nothing.

If a company does not have enough cash to develop the product and market it, then it is either going to have to ask its shareholders for more money, or to do some deal (whether it be a joint venture or debt financing) that will effectively dilute the shareholders' stake in the product. And a company that does not have enough cash to see it through the next year is going to have to do something very quickly before it runs smack out of cash.

The tech stocks in the worst cash situation at the start of 2000 tended to be the small mining companies who had turned into dotcoms. Typically they didn't have much cash when they were miners and they had a bit less when they had transmuted into tech stocks. However, the veteran mining hands running these companies were inured to running without much cash and had some hope of survival. There was less hope among companies which had started with bundles of cash and whose technicians went on a spending spree on research.

The accounts will also include a balance sheet in which a value is put on the phone network, mastheads or Internet invention of a TMT company. My prejudices about these sorts of assets have already been mentioned. The value of the assets can be ascertained by turning to the profit and loss account. If the assets are not generating profits, they're not assets. If they're not generating profits now but will soon, it had better be very soon—like next year or, at most, the year after.

PREJUDICE 11

Content can be a nice asset, a cable or other distribution network can be a nice asset, but any invention that needs continuous technological development can turn into an ugly asset.

Let's say Saw-Toothed Software is a company developing an application which will download data ten times faster than any other application can right now. As far as we know good old Saw-Toothed Software is right at the cutting-edge. State of the art. Whoopee! Only trouble is, somewhere around the globe—Silicon Valley, India, wherever—some nerd is working on an application that will download data 1000 times faster. Saw-Toothed Software may get to the market first, but the odds with any technological breakthrough is that the window will be short-lived before a rival developer comes up with something better. Let's say Saw-Toothed Software actually steps on the pedal and manages to market its software to IBM, Microsoft and the rest of the gang. The Indians in India or Silicon Valley are still working their butts off and will come up with a far faster system soon. So what does Saw-Toothed Software have to do? It has to keep spending on research and development to stay ahead of the

50 THE NUMBERS GAME

Indians. However much money it reaps from selling its initial invention to the big boys, it's going to have to reinvest heaps more to stay ahead.

PREJUDICE 12

Software development companies may get a bonanza from the original software, but in the long term (which may be one year in this industry) future development will be necessary and that means the software will have to be owned by someone with *deeeeep* pockets.

In the 1990s, some companies such as Microsoft and Cisco Systems had grown from atoms into a whole universe and made fortunes for anyone who had the vision to buy their stock in the early days and hold it. The same could be said for anyone who bought a parcel of News shares in the fledgling days of Rupert Murdoch. Anyone who has the insight to pick a stock that is going to become a master of the universe doesn't need to read this book or anything much else.

At any given time in the share market there are probably minnows that are going to grow into whale sharks. Usually there are only one or two such minnows. The current boom may have spawned more than usual (which appears to be the case in the USA) but the failure rate will still be high. If you've found the next Microsoft, close this book and start checking the real estate prices on the Riviera. But if your stock doesn't happen to be the next Microsoft then one day it is going to have to conform to the old-fashioned norms of P/E ratios and—unlikely as it seems—dividend yields.

Retailers

Mass market retailers operate on relatively thin margins, so they have to be as efficient as possible. Consider the profit-to-sales ratio from 1995 to 2002 for Australia's largest retailing group, Coles Myer (as shown in Table 3.1).

Table 3.1 Coles Myer profit-to-sales analysis

Year	2002	2001	2000	1999	1998	1997	1996	1995
Sales ($m)	25 689	23 799	24 168	22 438	20 588	19 225	18 175	16 802
EBIT ($m)	624	586	826	751	674	615	578	730
NPAT ($m)	354	333	483	405	368	389	280	423
EBIT/Sales	2.4%	2.5%	3.4%	3.3%	3.3%	2.6%	3.2%	4.3%
NPAT/Sales	1.4%	1.4%	2.0%	1.8%	1.8%	2.0%	1.5%	2.5%

As the table shows, in 1998 Coles Myer made just 3.3 cents EBIT margin on each dollar's worth of goods they sold—and that was before paying interest and tax. After interest and tax the net profit margin shrank to 1.8 cents in the dollar. To put it another way, every time a shoplifter stole a $1 bar of soap that year, the group had to sell another 55 to get square. So now you know why the big retailers don't like shoplifters.

The second point is that Coles Myer's margins have varied widely over the five years. If in 1999 they could have maintained the 4.3 per cent EBIT margin of 1995, EBIT would have risen by $224 million. That would have been a 30 per cent jump. On the other hand, if margins had stayed at the 1997 level of 2.6 per cent, EBIT in 1999 would have been down by $167 million—a 22 per cent fall. Tiny movements in operating margin make a huge difference to retailers.

Readers will note that sales growth appears quite strong through the eight years. It's not quite as strong as it looks, because the chain was opening more stores each year. In 1995 Coles Myer had 1787 stores. By 1999 the figure had grown to 2027. The strong sales growth becomes less impressive when shown on a per-store basis. But margins began declining seriously in 2001 and 2002, even though sales held up reasonably well.

This again underlines the supreme importance of efficiency in large retail chains. They are under constant pressure to keep sales up and costs down. There are two calculations by which this efficiency can be measured. They are the stock-turn ratio and sales per square metre.

We met the stock-turn ratio when analysing the Amcor accounts. It is calculated by finding the average of stock at the

52 THE NUMBERS GAME

start and finish of the year and dividing the figure into sales (refer to Table 3.2).

Table 3.2 Coles Myer stock-turn ratio

Year	2002	2001	2000	1999	1998	1997
Average inventory ($m)	2 856.6	2 911.0	2 891.5	2 733.3	2 562.8	2 425.0
Sales ($m)	25 689.0	23 799.0	24 168.0	22 438.1	20 587.6	19 224.8
Stock-turn ratio	9.0 times	8.2 times	8.4 times	8.2 times	8.0 times	7.9 times

The faster a company can turn over its stock, the better it should perform. In 1999 and 1998 Coles Myer showed a fractional improvement in performance by turning over stock a little quicker. In 2002, Coles Myer showed a substantial increase in stock turnover, but as can be seen from Table 3.1, its profit margins did not improve and were low by historical standards. That tells us its margins were really under pressure. Although it was churning stock faster, its overall margins were the same, so the margin per item was falling. This ratio can be manipulated by altering inventory levels at balance date by shipping goods back to suppliers (or by telling the suppliers to hold back shipments), but in a group the size of Coles Myer that would take a lot of transport. In smaller retailers inventory figures can also be misleading for other reasons. If a store sells a pair of shoes at balance date and the customer brings them back the next day because they pinch around the toes, then an item that has been moved out of inventory will have to go back in, or be written off. If a couple buy a refrigerator on credit, the store will mark it off inventory and the outstanding debt becomes a receivable. But if the couple then default on the payments, the store may have to repossess the refrigerator.

This became a great problem in retail chains in the 1950s. In those days the stores were anxious to maintain sales figures by any device. H.G. Palmer would offer a trade-in price of, say, £10 (as it was then) on your old refrigerator to sell a new one for £50. The company would chalk up the full profit on the refrigerator it had sold and take the trade-in into inventory at £10. But the trade-in was never sold because nobody would have bought it at the price. So Palmers developed a warehouse full of unsaleable old refrigerators—and other goods—which were never depreciated from the inventory. This was a major cause of its ultimate collapse in 1963. Palmer's auditor went to prison— and so he should have.

Back to modern times and Coles Myer. The other number for measuring retail efficiency is sales per square metre of floor space (see Table 3.3). Any retailer worth its salt should disclose this number, which has been a standard measure for a long time.

Table 3.3 Coles Myer sales per square metre

Year	2002	2001	2000	1999	1998	1997	1996	1995	1944
Selling area (sqm)	2 575	2 571	2 577	3 797	3 673	3 526	3 461	3 376	3 284
Sales ($m)	25 689	23 799	24 168	22 438	20 588	19 225	18 175	16 802	15 921
Sales per sqm ($)	9 976	9 256	9 378	5 909	5 605	5 452	5 251	4 976	4 847

Quite a creditable performance. Coles Myer had managed to increase its sales per square metre every year until 2001. The expansion into liquor from 2000 explains the jump in figures from that date. But note again that despite this increase in efficiency, Coles Myer was unable to improve its margins.

Retailing is a tough, low-margin business. The retailers who succeed tend to be veterans with a successful track record, notably Paul Simons in his days at Woolworths.

Gaming companies

Casinos (watch the win rates)

A well-run casino is about statistical probabilities and not about much else. A roulette wheel is a good example. The wheel has 36 numbers. If you bet on any one of them and win, the casino will pay you at odds of 35 to 1. If you bet on the black, you have eighteen numbers running for you and the casino will pay even money.

But there is also a zero on the wheel and that will come up

once in every 37 spins. When the zero comes up the house rakes in all bets on the board. In French, the language of roulette, this house advantage is called the 'cagnotte' and amounts to a commission of 2.7 per cent.

The random nature of an unrigged roulette wheel means that zero could come up three times in a row or never in 100 spins, but over time it will come up once in every 37. The more times the wheel is spun, the closer the occurrence of zero will conform to that frequency. That is a statistical certainty.

Note that the house take is not reduced even if the gamblers are allowed to bet on zero. That is because it is still paying only 35 to 1 in a game where the real odds are 36 to 1. For every time the house pays out at 35 to 1 on zero, it has collected 36 times.

The gamblers on the wheel may be getting a rush from the glamour of their surroundings or the thrill of wagering or alcohol or all three. The house, on the other side of the wheel, is devoid of emotion. It mechanically collects the cagnotte, draining the gamblers' capital slightly every time they spin. The more often the roulette wheel spins, the more certain its percentage take becomes.

The odds on every game in the casino are set in the house's favour. Otherwise there wouldn't be a casino (although an amazing number of punters seem to ignore that elementary fact). So it makes more sense to hold casino shares than to play the tables.

There are basically two kinds of business in Australian casinos: the grind and the high rollers. The definition of high rollers varies a bit, but generally they are prepared to lose a minimum of $100 000. If you're not in this league, you're part of the grind.

The grind business is the bread and butter of any casino. The small players who patronise the tables and gaming machines are bound to lose overall. The hordes who play the gaming machines either don't know or don't care that the average payout ratio is around 90 per cent, so that for every $100 they put through they lose $10.[2] The percentage that the house will win from its grind players is highly predictable, and depends mainly on the mix of games and machines. High roller business is rather different. Firstly, the high rollers have to be bribed before they will turn up. They are offered discount or free air fares and accommodation. In return they undertake to turn over a set amount on the tables.

The reward for the casino is that if the high rollers are unlucky they can lose an awful lot of money to the house very quickly. The risk for the casino is that the various bribes and discounts offered to the high rollers may wipe out any profits the casino makes. If the discounts offered are too heavy and the high rollers get lucky, the casino may make heavy losses on them.

So high rollers can be lucrative for a casino but they need very careful management. One of the great problems is limits. Casino win rates are based on the premises that: (a) players will bet around the same amount on each game; and (b) that they will stay at the table for a reasonable period of time. But the players can shift those odds dramatically. Let's say a player has been going for an hour at $10 000 a hand at baccarat and is down $100 000. If the player is allowed to lift his limit to $100 000 he can get square in a single hand.

The house take on baccarat, the game most favoured by high rollers, is 1.25 per cent. That means for every $100 million bet by high rollers, the house should collect $1.25 million in EBITDA (earnings before interest, tax, depreciation and amortisation). If they play other games as well, the house odds improve a bit.

The whole point about casino stocks is that the win rates on both the grind and high roller businesses will in time converge to the theoretical win rate. In the September quarter of 1998, for example, Crown announced EBITDA of $53 million. Crown, quite properly, went on to point out that its win rate on high rollers had been 1.6 per cent compared to the theoretical rate of 1.28 per cent on this business, which would have reduced EBITDA to $48.5 million.

Crown investors should have taken the theoretical rate as their best guide, because sooner or later the win rates average out. The iron logic of this is that if the win rates are fixed over time, the profits earned by the casino will vary only for the following reasons.

Higher volume The higher the turnover of the casino, the higher the revenue because the win rate will stay the same. Of course, if a casino is already operating at maximum capacity it will be difficult to increase turnover.

Bad management If the business is being managed badly, the win rate will fall.

Cost control If the casino spends too much attracting punters, they will erode the win rate. Australian casinos compete for the custom of high rollers, offering free accommodation, free air fares, free booze and food and various other enticements. If the enticements get too luxurious, they will erode the win rate on the high rollers. And, of course, occasionally a high roller gets lucky and skins the casino.

Good management is revealed through its track record over time. However, one still needs to watch for 'normalising' of results. In the December half of 2001, for example, PBL announced a profit of $183.5 million, fractionally higher than that for the previous corresponding period. Closer examination showed this headline number had been normalised to reflect what the profit would have been if the win rate had been normal. Instead of the normal 1.28 per cent win rate on high rollers it had slipped to 1.09 per cent during the half. The actual profit had been $160 million, which was down 17 per cent on the previous December half. Sure enough, Crown's win rate returned in succeeding periods, but investors should always stick to the actual profit rather than the normalised, because a fall in the win rate could reflect deteriorating management.

Gaming machines

A licence to print money by any company that owns them. Gaming machines used to be called 'one-armed bandits' in the old days when players pulled a handle to operate them. Modern electronic machines have lost the handle but they're still bandits. Anyone who doubts this only needs to look at the results they yield for gaming companies.

As at June 1999, Tabcorp operated 13 690 gaming machines in Victoria plus another 622 in Queensland. Those 14 312 machines produced EBIT of $176.4 million, which equates to $12 325 per machine.

The only risk for any company owning or operating gaming machines is that their franchise might be lost or impaired. Concerns about gambling addiction in Australia were raised by a Productivity Commission inquiry in 1999, but little action seemed likely to be taken. Cynics will have noted that state and territory governments who derive enormous revenue from gaming are as addicted to it as the worst gamblers.

Wagering

The term wagering used to mean betting on racehorses, pacers and greyhounds, but has now been widened to include all forms of sport betting, particularly football. As long as the gaming companies operate pure totalisators, in which the commission is deducted before dividing the pool of bets amongst the winners, this is risk-free. However, gaming companies are now beginning to offer fixed-price betting in some forms of wagering, which has the capacity to increase risk.

Broadly, gaming companies are low-risk operations as long as those who own casinos have them under tight control. Also, they are controlled and audited so tightly by governmental authorities that the numbers in their accounts should be pretty reliable. The year-on-year numbers should reflect any significant variations in their business, giving investors a good feel for whether their company is performing well or badly. Anecdotal evidence indicates that gambling in Australia must be getting closer to saturation point, which may mean that future growth in gaming companies' profits will be small unless (in the case of casinos) they can attract increasing numbers of foreign high rollers.

So the main points about gaming companies are:

- The win rate is mainly applicable to high rollers. Significant variation above 1.28 per cent should be regarded as temporary. Significant variation below 1.28 per cent, if sustained, points to poor management.
- Just think about that Crown win rate of 1.28 per cent for a

58 THE NUMBERS GAME

second. On one side of the table is a punter hoping to get lucky. On the other side, the casino has calculated its win rate to two decimal points. No prizes for guessing who will win in the long haul provided management is efficient.

- The grind business in casinos should show a steady percentage return.
- Keep an eye on the operating margins, and the trend in those margins. That should reflect what sort of job the management is doing. A well-run casino or TAB should show steady growth in margins due to efficiency and cost control.
- If the figures are available, calculate the earnings per machine and per table. Again, they should show steady growth.

Once a gaming company has gone through its teething stages and good management has been installed, it should become highly profitable and its accounts should be easy to analyse.

The biggest risk to these companies is not in the numbers but in variations which governments may make to their franchises, either to squeeze them harder for tax revenue or to protect chronic gamblers from their addiction.

Insurance companies

(Warning: Readers not possessing strong powers of concentration should skip this one.)

The accounts of insurance companies are among the hardest for an outsider to analyse. A shareholder simply has no way of knowing whether an insurer has got its potential liabilities right or not. Shareholders who are prepared to do some really heavy detective work back in the notes to accounts can make an educated guess. Australian accounting standard AASB 1038 (which applies to all life insurance company accounts from 31 December 1999) has shed a little light in the dark places, and we will be leaning heavily upon that to make sense of the numbers in life insurers. The recent collapse of HIH and the post mortem has proved conclusively that if a general insurer wants to fudge its accounts, no outsider has a hope in hell of discovering the truth.

TYPES OF COMPANIES 59

Amendments to the law proposed by the HIH Royal Commission may improve the situation, but that is yet to be seen.[3]

Insurance is all about the laws of probability and the shareholder should always remember that those laws were discovered by Galileo when he had been commissioned by Italian gamblers to work out which numbers were most likely to recur in a dice game.

Insurance is a gamble and the best insurers are the ones who would make the best bookmakers because they have the most accurate assessment of their risks and returns. An insurance policy is a promise to pay if some defined event happens (death, car accident, house fire, and so on). The insurer collects a premium (which can be taken as a bet by the customer) and will pay out when and if the defined event happens—presuming the insurer cannot escape through the various weasel clauses they all put in their contracts.

The premium varies depending on the risk. A 30-year-old man is obviously a safer bet for a life policy than a 70-year-old, and a 30-year-old woman is an even better bet. Occasionally a 30-year-old gets hit by a bus the day after he signs the policy, but the more 30-year-olds and 70-year-olds an insurance company has on its books, the closer their life expectancies will conform to the statistical norm and the more accurately the insurer should be able to assess its future payouts and thereby frame its book.

Actuaries spend their lives studying statistics, working out the probabilities of house theft in Dandenong as compared to Toorak, the incidence of cancer in smokers against non-smokers, and so on. The insurance companies set their premiums according to the actuaries' calculations. These premiums form a big ball of cash which the company invests until the day when it has to pay out.

Broadly, there are two types of insurance—life insurance (which would more accurately be named death insurance)—and general insurance (auto, fire, product liability and the rest). In Australia it has generally been the case that general insurers make losses on their insurance underwriting (that is, their payouts each year exceed their premium income) but these are more than offset by the investment income and so the insurer makes a profit. This is sometimes true of life insurance companies too,

60 THE NUMBERS GAME

but the profit of a life insurance company is the product of a considerable number of assumptions, which we shall visit shortly.

Life insurance

The old saying among life salesmen is: 'I can sell you the perfect policy if you can tell me exactly when you plan to die.' But on actuarial averages, he knows the most likely date. Or to be more exact, he is selling a policy designed to the mathematics of an actuary who does know the most likely date.[4] So, as we noted earlier, the company accepts the premiums each year while storing up a ball of cash to meet its payouts later on. For a typical life company let's examine AMP's 1999 accounts. When reading them, it is worth remembering that AMP suffered a disaster in 2002–03 but that was because it was selling products in the UK with guaranteed returns at a time when its investments were primarily in equities. That was good business for a while, but AMP failed to pick the turn in the equity markets, where the FTSE100 index in the UK fell by 50 per cent in three years. Nothing in AMP's accounts could have enabled investors to forecast what was going to happen. However, the following remarks should help you to analyse life company accounts in years when a market wipeout isn't happening.

Time to look at the balance sheet on the next page.[5] Try not to flinch.

The good news is that you can ignore the small numbers. Just concentrate on the biggies. Typically, the asset side of an insurance company balance sheet will be dominated by investments. In the case of AMP, they comprise $100 billion in debt and equity securities. The liabilities side will be dominated by the company's estimate of the current value of its future payouts. (Technically, this is called a liability for outstanding claims and is defined as the present value of expected future payments.) This outstanding claims liability is the most critical number in any insurer's accounts. If it is too low, the company will be overstating its profits and if it's too big the company will be understating them. Unfortunately, even with the best will in the world it is possible for the actuaries to be wrong in making any of

TYPES OF COMPANIES **61**

Table 3.4 AMP balance sheet, 31 December 1999

	$m
Assets	
Cash	6 208
Outstanding premiums	925
Receivables	4 028
Equity securities	58 120
Debt securities	42 536
Property	13 224
Other investments	1 719
Operating assets	591
Excess of market value over net assets of controlled entities	2 659
Other assets	1 230
Total assets	**131 240**
Liabilities	
Accounts payable	(2 084)
Unearned premium	(1 161)
Outstanding claims	(5 385)
Borrowings	(9 607)
Provisions	(6 182)
Policy owner liabilities	(88 337)
Unvested policy owner benefits	(1 150)
Subordinated debt	(2 062)
Total liabilities	**(115 968)**
Net assets	**15 272**

the several estimates upon which this figure is based. In the case of AMP we are looking at $88 billion, which is serious money.

In everything that follows, it is worth remembering that AMP's stated operating revenue for 1999 was $27 billion and its operating profit before abnormal items and tax was $2.4 billion. So if that estimate of $88 billion outstanding claims liability is out by a mere 2.7 per cent either way, the operating profit would have been either doubled or wiped out.

So it's important to know how AMP reached the $88 billion figure. This was summarised in Note 21 to the accounts, which is reproduced in Table 3.5.

62 THE NUMBERS GAME

Table 3.5 Calculating the value of AMP's liabilities, 1999

	$m	
Policy owner liabilities		
Valued by projection method		
a Best estimate		
Value of future policy benefits	57 577	
Value of future expenses	5 273	
Value of future premiums	(17 923)	
Total		**44 907**
b Value of future profits		
Policy owners' bonuses	19 061	
Shareholders' profit margins	5 320	
Total		**24 381**
Valued by accumulation method		
a Best estimate		
Value of future policy benefits	17 058	
Future charges for acquisition expenses	(40)	
Total		**17 018**
b Value of declared bonus		1 583
Net policy owner liabilities		87 889
Policy liabilities ceded under reinsurance		448
Total		**88 337**

Margin on services Table 3.5 is calculated using what is called margin on services (MoS) methodology. Margin on services is designed to recognise profits on a life insurance policy as the services on that policy are performed and the income received. Profits are deferred and amortised over the life of the policy, whereas losses are recognised immediately they arise. In general terms, policy liability is the present value of all future expected payments, expenses and profit margins reduced by the value of all future expected premiums. AMP complicates the issue enormously by using two separate methods for determining liabilities—the projection and accumulation methods. For life business, it primarily uses the projection method and the accumulation method is mostly used for investment-linked business.

It's probably best to skip the actuarial lore that projection and accumulation carry in their train and say that the policy liabilities are the amounts which, when taken together with future premiums and investment earnings, are required to meet the payment of future benefits and expenses. They are also discounted back to present values to allow for inflation.

The first line in Table 3.5 shows the value of future policy benefits. This is the total amount AMP expects to pay out on its policies in future years. It is calculated after studying mortality rates and risk factors and then discounting back for inflation to reach a net present value. Note there are two separate calculations of future policy payouts, one calculated by projection and the second by accumulation.

AMP also takes into account the value of future expenses, such as administration and salespeople's commissions. From these are deducted the inflow of premiums paid by the customers.

AMP must also calculate the future profits its investments will generate. Once that profit is calculated, it is allocated between policyholders' bonuses and profits attributable to shareholders. So the line in the table that reads shareholders' profit margins is the one that tells us what AMP expects its future profits to be, at net present valuation. And at the bottom of the table we see the figure of $88 billion, as it appears in the balance sheet.

So far, so good. But if we're in a cynical mood, are there any tricks or traps we can look for that might indicate whether an insurance company has got its figures right or wrong? The short answer is no, because we are dealing in probabilities rather than absolutes. But tracking through the jungle of notes to accounts, we might pick up a few clues as to whether a company has been optimistic or conservative in its valuations.

Discount rates Discount rates are not all cut and dried. Different companies may use different discount rates to reach their numbers for present liabilities. Given that we are dealing in very large numbers which compound over many years, a 0.5 per cent differential in discount rates could easily produce a difference of a billion dollars or so in the present value of policyholders' liabilities. Some insurance companies publish the discount numbers they use and it's worth checking them. Because the numbers typically cover a range, a shareholder will still not be able to

64 THE NUMBERS GAME

make an exact comparison but he or she will at least get a feel for the relative conservatism of the various companies. Table 3.6 shows AMP's discount rates for 1998 and 1999.

Table 3.6 Insurance company discount rates

AMP	1999	1998
Non-linked business	5.8%/8.4%	4.4%/6.4%
Linked business	6.2%/8.9%	4.6%/6.6%

Official interest rates rose by an average of about 1 per cent in the calendar years of 1998 and 1999, whereas the range of AMP's rates rose by between 1.4 per cent and 2.3 per cent. It would thus appear that AMP was being more conservative in its 1999 accounts than in 1998. From a shareholder's viewpoint, conservatism is a mixed blessing. Conservatism is good, because it means the company is in less danger of making losses or going broke. It's bad because it decreases the declared profit and hence the dividends. On the whole, it's probably better to have a company that's a little conservative and will be here next year. Okay, let's look at a few more features of life company accounts.

What belongs to the shareholders? Looking again at the balance sheet (Table 3.4), AMP has some $131 billion in assets and $116 billion in liabilities, so its net assets are $15 billion, right?

Not quite. In fact, the liabilities to policy owners are just what they say they are. The $88 billion represents AMP's best estimate of the present value of what it would have to pay its policyholders as at the end of the second millennium. That sum should be regarded as funds held in trust for the policyholders. The money will belong to the policyholders eventually and not the company. The same can be said for the $1150 million worth of unvested policy owner benefits on the next line. These are amounts owed to participating policyholders who, as the name suggests, have a right to participate in AMP profits.[6]

So a total of $89 487 million of AMP's liabilities were to policyholders and exactly the same amount of assets should be attributed to them. If we subtract that sum from both sides of the balance sheet we find that AMP at the end of 1999 had total assets of \$41 753 million and total liabilities of \$26 481 million. The figure for net assets remains exactly the same at \$15 272 million, but as far as shareholders in the company are concerned any ratio calculations should be done with the second set of figures and not the first.

Consolidating life company accounts When the accounts of a manufacturing company and its subsidiaries are consolidated into one set of numbers, the methodology for all the companies is the same. All the subsidiaries' assets and liabilities are simply added to the parent company's, with internal transactions eliminated. Not so with life companies.

The standard AASB 1038 provides that a life company must value all of its assets at market value. If Life Company A owns Life Company B, Company B has to be held in Company A's accounts at market value. This is part of what is called the mark-to-market rule. But if a non-life company owns Life Company B the accounts can simply be consolidated in the same manner as with a manufacturing company.

Mark-to-market means that a company must value all its assets at current market values, which sounds realistic but can be a pain in the neck. If AMP is holding Commonwealth bonds with a face value of \$1000 and which are due to mature in four years' time, a rise in interest rates may depress their current value to \$950 at balance date, so AMP has to mark them down to that value. It matters not that AMP has no intention of selling the bonds until maturity, when they will be worth \$1000. Mark-to-market is also called appraisal value.

Appraisal value Appraisal value? This is an actuarial valuation of the company's embedded value (which we'll get to in a few pages) plus the value of new business. So if a company is valued at appraisal, we need to look carefully at how that appraisal was done. Has the valuation been done aggressively or conservatively? And, not unimportantly, has the method of valuation changed since last year?

The appraisal value of a company can be basically described as the extrapolation of its present trends. The actuary looks at the profitability of the existing business and of new business

66 THE NUMBERS GAME

being written and extrapolates that trend into the future, after allowing for the capital that will need to be tied up in the business. But there is no hard and fast rule as to how far in the future one should extrapolate new business. This can make a huge difference. If the profitability of new business is $50 million currently and that is extrapolated out ten years, then the appraisal value of the business is $500 million. But if it is extrapolated out twenty years, the value—after applying discount factors—could be $800 million. Broadly, ten years is regarded as a conservative valuation and twenty years as an aggressive valuation.

These appraisal valuations incorporate a discount rate. There are two views as to what comprises a valid discount rate. Some analysts discount it by what an investor would reasonably expect to earn as a return on assets over the period, after allowing for the risk rating of the various assets in the portfolio. Others use a margin above the ten-year bond rate. Discount rates tend to be driven by interest rates and might vary anywhere between 11 per cent and 15 per cent.

The allowance for future capital requirements also needs a word of explanation. Every time a life company writes a new policy, it has to set aside an amount of capital to meet its solvency requirements (which means to cover its future obligations). That capital then has to be monitored. If the company is earning only 8 per cent on its capital when the policy requires a rate of 10 per cent to keep it serviced, then the company will have to increase the amount of capital committed to the policy. The appraisal value calculation takes this factor into account.

This means, by the way, that when an insurance company is expanding its business rapidly, it will have to commit more capital to meet its solvency requirements. This can be a real drag on rapid expansion. In the late 1980s Westpac plunged into insurance and did brilliantly. However, the rapid expansion of the business caused a heavy drain of capital at a time when Westpac was in diabolical trouble in various parts of its banking business. So Westpac had to save itself by selling its insurance arm (probably its best business at the time) to AMP.

All pretty heavy going. The real message is that where a non-insurance holding company is consolidating one or more life companies into its group accounts, the holding company has considerable flexibility to horse around with the numbers, especially if it's using appraisal values. Changing from consolidation of net asset values to appraisal values can boost both the balance sheet and the profit. To put it another way, the margin on services method of valuing life companies prevents them from bringing profits forward. The appraisal method encourages it. The shareholder needs to read notes to the accounts carefully—particularly note 1 on accounting policies—to discover what methods a company is using, and whether they have changed in the latest year.

The value of new business All these basics of insurance accounting are pretty stultifying stuff. Cutting to the chase, what an investor really needs to know is whether the company is doing better this year than last year. In the front of the annual report, the chairman will say of course it's doing better than last year. But does he know what he's talking about? And is there a way of checking?

The answer is yes. But, as ever in insurance company accounting, we can't get to a final answer. We can, however, get a clue. The trend is shown in the value of future new business.

The concept is pretty simple. If a life company is writing policies at a loss, it's a bad proposition. If it's writing policies at a profit, it's a good proposition. Fortunately, by law there are now some numbers that give us a clue as to which is the case. The numbers are hidden deep in the notes to accounts, but they are worth hunting down. If the company shows the numbers right up front, of course, maybe they've really got something to brag about.

For an example, let's go to Colonial Limited. The graph (shown here as Figure 3.1) from page 30 of Colonial's 1999 annual report shows the value of the latest year's new insurance business. Australian new business is good and improving, up to about $23 million. Asia is fantastic at nearly $30 million. New Zealand has made a big rebound to nearly $10 million. The UK has been a disaster area, but is climbing out of the hole and now has a negative value of only $17 million. The net of these figures is $46 million. Applying a conservative multiple of ten, that gives us an appraisal value of $460 million for Colonial's new insurance business. In fact, that might be a bit too conservative. The

Figure 3.1 Value of one year's new business — insurance operations

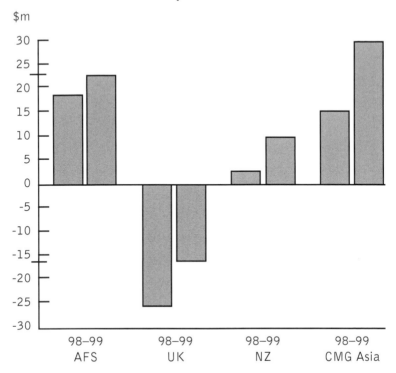

UK business is so far in the red that no self-respecting insurer could tolerate writing business at those losses for long. This is evidenced, after a fashion, by the fact the losses are diminishing. So let's put the UK on a six multiple and leave the rest on ten. That would lift our appraisal value to $528 million.

These are the profits we expect to be reported in future years, net of the liabilities that fall due in those years. The appraisal value takes everything up front.

Hunting the notes Is there a way of checking these numbers? Sort of. The margin on services method calculates a profit to shareholders on the business. It is calculated from the following components.

- Expected or planned profits. At the time of writing a policy, best-estimate assumptions are used to determine all expected

future payments and premiums. These expected profit margins are released over the life of the policy.
- Experienced profits or losses. These are realised where actual experience differs from expected performance. Maybe people start living longer, or expenses rise.
- Recognised losses less reversals of prior year losses. This happens when a company trying to capture market share writes new business which is expected to produce returns below the prevailing discount rate. Revised estimates might lead to a write-off of future profits that have previously been brought to book. Or, if the company gets lucky, it may be able to reverse prior losses.
- Investment earnings on shareholder capital and retained earnings. (The company had a better year on the market than it expected).

It is best explained by illustration. Deep back on page 100 of the Colonial accounts for 1999 was the following little table (shown here as Table 3.7). This gives us a better picture, although not the full one. Looking at 1999 first, the top line shows the expected profit in each region. Looking at the operating margin line, Australia did much better than expected, New Zealand came in close to target, while the UK and Asia performed badly. Investment earnings pushed them all up considerably, particularly Australia and the UK. Remember that 1999 was a particularly good year on the share market for most stocks. If we compare this table with the earlier graph on new business, the UK looks a little healthier but Asia looks more dubious.

Now let's look at the comparison with 1998. That shows us Australia's going gangbusters. The planned profit margin rose in 1999 and the operating margin was up even further. Terrific. New Zealand improved remarkably. Great. The UK reduced its planned profit margins but was still writing new business below cost to the tune of $12 million. Better than the corresponding loss of $22 million in 1998, but it still needed to improve. Asia's operating margin was no better in 1999 but it had stepped up its expected profit and its investment earnings were running strongly. These tables give us the best feel in the accounts for

70 THE NUMBERS GAME

Table 3.7 MoS shareholder profit analysis

	Australia $m	NZ $m	UK $m	Asia $m	Total $m
Colonial 1999					
Planned profit margins	62	25	32	22	141
Experience variation (new business losses)	28	(2)	(2)	(13)	11
Reversal of capitalised losses	16	—	(12)	(8)	(4)
Operating margins	106	23	18	1	148
Investment earnings	79	12	39	32	162
Net profit after tax	185	35	57	33	310
Colonial 1998					
Planned profit margins	32	7	37	11	87
Experience variation (new business losses)	14	(5)	(14)	(8)	(13)
Reversal of capitalised losses	3	(1)	(22)	(2)	(22)
Operating margins	49	1	1	1	52
Investment earnings	38	11	67	10	126
Net profit after tax	87	12	68	11	178

how a life company is running currently. Beware of one point, however. The line showing new business losses and reversals of capitalised losses is a net figure. The figure of $3 million for Australia in 1998, for example, could be the difference between write-offs of $18 million and a write-back of prior losses of $21 million. We just don't know. Unlike Salome, insurance companies never drop the last veil.

PREJUDICE 13

Steer clear of any insurance company which consistently produces adverse numbers on its new business. There be reefs and rocks about, me hearties.

Embedded value A phrase sometimes encountered when dealing with life insurance companies. Embedded value is an attempt to measure the value of the company to its shareholders. Embedded value comprises net assets plus the value of the company's existing contracts. Like just about every other important figure in life companies, it varies depending on discount rate assumptions. Table 3.8 shows the embedded value calculations for AMP as at December 1999.

Table 3.8 AMP Life statutory funds' embedded value, 1999 (all figures in $m)

Discount margin	4%	5%	6%	7%
Shareholders' net assets	1 988	1 988	1 988	1 988
Value of in-force business	4 345	4 101	3 883	3 690
Embedded value	6 333	6 089	5 871	5 678

The risk discount rates in this case are the risk discount margin plus the yield on Australian ten-year bonds. If the embedded value figure is not given, there is normally no way a lay reader can calculate it because insurance companies do not always show the figure for the value of in-force business, nor the figure for the shareholders' net assets in the life business as opposed to other elements of the company's business. If the figure cannot be found or calculated the best advice is probably not to worry about it. If an investor can't get a rough idea of how a life company is performing from the other tips in this section, embedded value won't help him much. The embedded value calculation usually becomes important only when a company is under takeover threat.

Solvency reserves The solvency reserve is a figure set by regulators to ensure that life insurance companies hold prudential reserves over and above their policy liabilities, as a buffer against adverse experience and poor investment returns. So even if the company is having higher payouts than expected and doing poorly on the share market, its commitments will still be honoured. Table 3.9 shows Colonial's solvency reserves for the various companies under its umbrella in 1999, and the assets it held to cover those reserves.

72 THE NUMBERS GAME

Table 3.9 Colonial group solvency reserves, 1999

	Col Fiji Life	Col Mut Life	Col Fin Corp	Col Life NZ	Col Life UK	CMG Asia Life	CMG Asia Ins Inc
Solvency reserve	11	621	118	67	282	239	1
Assets available	20	988	233	72	1 348	273	15
Cover (times)	1.8	1.6	2.0	1.1	4.8	1.1	15.0

The solvency reserves are usually set at fairly conservative levels by the various regulators. Except in abnormal conditions, companies should not need to hold a large buffer above the reserve. It would be roughly equivalent to a bank holding too much cash. For some reason the UK arm of Colonial seemed to be holding too many reserve assets at the end of 1999.

General insurance

Insurance is basically a promise. A properly run insurance company (let's call it Perfect Insurance) collects premiums from its customers in return for a promise to pay if a certain event occurs in the future. To ensure it will be able to meet that promise, Perfect pitches its premiums at an adequate level to cover the risks. As the premiums are collected up front, Perfect has a growing ball of cash to invest between the time it collects and when—if ever—it pays out. Perfect invests these premiums as well as possible. It therefore has two streams of income—from premiums and investments—to cover its future payments.

To ensure that its future liabilities will be met, Perfect should take a conservative view of them. When you look at an insurer's balance sheet, the largest item on the asset side will be investments. As the company collects premiums, they are invested in bonds, equities and property. On the liabilities side, the largest item is entitled 'outstanding liabilities', which is the company's estimate of the present value of what it will have to pay out on future claims.

How does the company estimate that amount? Well, that's where we meet the actuary. The easiest way to think of an actuary is as a bookmaker. Before a race meeting a bookie sets the odds against the horses so that maybe he lays the book to 110 per cent. That is, if there are 11 horses in the race and each is backed to win $1000, his maximum payout will be $10 000 and the other $1000 is his profit.

An actuary does exactly the same thing for an insurance company. Let's take the old NRMA Insurance, now Insurance Australia Group, as an example. They insure cars against theft or accident. They have years of statistics on the percentage of cars which have accident claims in Sydney and the average cost per claim. They also have years of statistics on the trends in accident claims and payouts.

Armed with these figures a half-bright actuary should be able to make a pretty accurate central estimate of the global amount IAG will pay out in car accident claims next year. That means, in turn, that the company should be able to set its premiums accurately. And the company should have similarly accurate figures and be able to make a central estimate on theft.

Central estimate is an important concept. If the central estimate for accident claims in Sydney next year is, say, $100 million, that means there is a 50 per cent probability of the actual number being either higher or lower. It's a median, if you like. Industry practice is to start with that median, or central, estimate and to add a bit more protection to it. So having made the central estimate, the company might add a prudential margin of 15 per cent and lift that $100 million figure to $115 million. Alternatively, the company might make a more conservative estimate so that there's a 75 per cent probability that the number of claims will be lower but only a 25 per cent risk that they will be higher. That can be thought of as another form of prudential margin.

There is still a chance in any given year that the claims will actually turn out to be higher than even the conservative estimate, but the probability of that happening is low because our Perfect Insurance has given itself a reasonable margin and, over time, the statistics will conform to the long-term trend.

Does that leave Perfect Insurance with any risk? Yes, there could be a major hailstorm such as the one that hit Sydney's eastern suburbs on 19 April 1999 which damages an abnormally large number of cars in a single event.

74 THE NUMBERS GAME

But that's easily covered. All Perfect Insurance has to do is take out reinsurance covering it for any single event in which more than, say, $5 million in damages is incurred. That's called outwards reinsurance and would typically be split between many insurance companies all around the world. Once it's done that, Perfect Insurance should be covered for all risks. Its management could spend a lot of time on the golf course, content in the knowledge the money was steadily rolling in. The old NRMA Insurance made very good profits, particularly because its road service division gave it a strongly loyal customer base. Working in this way, an insurance company should be able to make a comfortable living insuring cars, houses and other short-tail business, short-tail generally meaning any policy where the claim should arise within a year of the event.

The steps which an actuary is supposed to take when estimating the insurer's liabilities to its policyholders are set out under AASB 1023. For the record, here are the three main steps:

1   The actuaries have to estimate how many successful claims are going to arise from business currently on the company's books. These will include unpaid reported claims, claims incurred but not reported (IBNR), adjustments for claims development, claims incurred but not enough reported (IBNER) and costs expected to be incurred in settling claims. In life business, this involves making assumptions about mortality rates. In general business, it involves making assumptions about frequency of auto accidents, home fires, workers' compensation and so forth. These estimates depend upon the company knowing the degree of risk attached to each of the types of business it insures. If the insurer has written too much house insurance in north Queensland, for example, it might be vulnerable to cyclone damage. If it has written too many life policies on smokers or asbestosis victims, they might die earlier than expected. The actuaries also have to estimate their outstanding liabilities on reinsurance business, which we will deal with later.

   Claims IBNR arise from events known to have happened which will give rise to claims which have not yet been received. (NRMA Insurance knew the moment the great

Sydney hailstorm of April 1999 struck that it was going to receive claims, for instance.) Claims expense and outstanding claim liability must be adjusted according to later information to reflect more accurately the cost of settlement. If the cost has been estimated wrongly because of court cases, price rises or other misjudgments, this represents claims IBNER.

2   These payouts will be offset by future earnings, so actuaries then have to estimate what the future rate of return on the company's investments will be. A small movement in the rate can make a huge difference to the numbers. If an insurer has a $1 billion investment portfolio, the decision to apply an 8 per cent rate of return as opposed to 7 per cent will cut $10 million a year, compounded, from the future liabilities. It will also have a dramatic impact on the profit declared in the current year.

3   As the future payouts will stretch over a long period, the actuaries then have to calculate what their present value will be. The liability for outstanding claims should reflect the amount which, if set aside at balance date, would accumulate to enough money to settle all claims as they fall due in the future. This involves two opposing calculations: inflating the amounts to determine future claim payments, then discounting back to measure the present value of those settlements. Again, a small movement in either the inflation or discount rate can have a very large impact on the future payout figure and hence the current year's profit.

When an insurer makes a big loss, it is almost always because it has made one of two mistakes, or possibly both.

The first mistake is under-provisioning. The big ball of cash sits on the asset side of the balance sheet. Deducted from it on the liabilities' side is the provision for future liabilities. That is the amount the actuaries reckon the insurer is going to pay out on the accidents, house fires and burglaries. Without knowing the basis of the actuaries' calculations, there is no way a shareholder—or even a fairly skilled analyst—can guess whether an insurance company is over- or under-provided. So insurance company accounts are inevitably opaque to outsiders. If an insurance company is under-providing, it is overstating its assets and profitability, and vice versa.

76 THE NUMBERS GAME

The second mistake is for a company to get its risk pricing wrong.

Note that the first and second mistakes are not exclusive. In fact, if a company is not getting its provisioning right there must always be a chance that it's not getting its risk pricing and spread right either, because the root cause of both mistakes is inadequate risk assessment.

The daddy of them all for inadequate risk assessment was HIH, which collapsed spectacularly in 2001. HIH historically tended to be large in professional indemnity and public liability insurance. That's long-tail and the difference from short-tail is important. An individual whose car is stolen or whose house is burned down gets on to the insurance company immediately. But someone who is the victim of legal malpractice or an industrial disease may not even discover the damage or the cause for years. There are asbestosis cases that date back two or three decades. Hence an insurer which offers long-tail coverage may never really know when to close the books on a policy. If an insurance company in long-tail business were honest when reporting its annual result, it would say: 'This is the profit we **think** we made last year, but we really won't know for another three or four years.'

That might be called a natural hazard of long-tail insurance. It was greatly exacerbated in the 1990s and early 2000s by a legal hazard. Once upon a time if a surfie dived into a sandbar on a public beach and broke his neck he'd think it was his own stupid fault. But under the modern, flourishing blame and claim industry, he will sue the local council or the lifesavers.

Damages claims began being admitted which a more robust society would previously have laughed out of court. Simultaneously, courts took it upon themselves to become substitutes for the social welfare system. Natural sympathy for the plight of some injured claimants translated into awards of $100 000, half a million and frequently more.

There was a syndrome abroad that such insurance payouts don't actually cost anyone anything. Our generous judges never seemed to stop for a second and wonder where the money comes from. An **occasional** big payout can be tolerated by the insurance industry without too much damage. When a **wholesale** trend of big payouts sets in, they have to get the money back either by raising premiums or narrowing coverage or both, all of which began happening in the wake of HIH's collapse (HIH having been the biggest price-cutter in the Australian market). Insurance companies tightened their game even further after the terrorist attacks on the World Trade Center in September 2001. Another factor was legislation by the NSW Government in 2002 which limited public liability payouts. All these factors combined to introduce a badly needed dose of reality into the insurance industry, both in Australia and overseas.

The collapse of HIH is worth exploring in a little detail, because it demonstrates just how meaningless an insurance company's accounts can be. HIH's last published accounts were for the year to June 2000 and were signed off on 16 October. The balance sheet showed shareholders' funds (net assets) of $939 million (or $927 million after outside interests). HIH closed its doors on 15 March, just five months after those accounts had been signed by the auditors, Arthur Andersen, as true and fair. The liquidator, Tony McGrath of KPMG, subsequently estimated that HIH had a deficiency of $3.6 billion on a central estimate and $5.3 billion on a conservative estimate. The latter figure would make it the largest loss in Australia's history.

Given the peculiar complexities of a large insurance liquidation, it was going to take at least a decade to determine the correct figure. Meanwhile, investors were left wondering how a set of accounts signed off by a top audit firm could be out by anywhere up to $6 billion within five months. One explanation is the divergence between the asset values of a going concern and those that prevail in a liquidation. But that only explained part of the divergence. The real story was that HIH had been systematically window-dressing its accounts for years. There was no major fraud in HIH but a lot of numbers were fudged to hide appallingly bad management mistakes and losses and eventually the whole edifice simply ran out of cash.

The prime mistake was that HIH was grabbing market share by charging lower premiums and taking higher risks. In any business, the surest way of going broke is by selling your product for less than it costs, which is what HIH was effectively doing. If any normal manufacturing company was doing that, it would go

78 THE NUMBERS GAME

out of business quickly. But in insurance there is a long time lag between receiving the premium and paying the claim. This time lag can be extended even further if the insurer refuses to pay claims by fighting them through the courts, delaying payment or simply ignoring the claimants, all of which HIH did.

HIH had been losing money for a long time before the liquidator arrived. Indeed, it appears to have been insolvent for years before the liquidator arrived. How did it disguise the fact it was broke? The answer is by a variety of artificial accounting stratagems.

Let's say, hypothetically, that in a particular year HIH collected $1 billion in premiums but an objective central estimate of the liabilities it took on would have been $1.2 billion. HIH therefore stood to lose $200 million on the business written that year. How did it manage to hide the $200 million loss for the year?

Well, it's not a cash loss, it's an estimated loss and that gives management a lot of room to horse around with the numbers, which depend on actuarial assumptions anyway. One tactic the company could use would be to take an optimistic view of claims and write them down accordingly. Another would be to write more business, so that incoming cash was greater than outgoing cash. In its desperation for new business, HIH kept cutting premiums, which meant that the more business it wrote, the more it was bound to lose when the chickens came home to roost. Another way would be by entering financial reinsurance contracts, which we will describe later. Yet another way would be to capitalise its expenses, which HIH did extensively. To illustrate the last of these techniques, consider the 2000 balance sheet of HIH shown in Table 3.10.

So HIH was claiming net assets of nearly a billion dollars when it was really a can of worms. An acute and sceptical reader could have unmasked some of the truth underlying these accounts. To begin with, the relationship of total assets to total liabilities is frightening. The $927 million attributable to HIH shareholders is a margin of only 12 per cent over total liabilities. That by itself should have been enough to send a perceptive shareholder racing to the phone to place a sell order. The ratio was particularly alarming in view of the fact that HIH had made

Table 3.10　HIH balance sheet, June 2000

	30.6.00 ($m)	30.6.99 ($m)
Current assets		
Cash	462	639
Receivables	1 604	1 401
Investments	624	804
Reinsurance recoveries	432	415
Deferred acquisition costs	304	278
Other	25	34
Total current assets	3 451	3 571
Non-current assets		
Receivables	1	35
Investments	1 753	1 909
Plant and equipment	165	148
Reinsurance recoveries	1 388	987
Intangibles	494	346
Other	244	192
Statutory funds	831	864
Total non-current assets	4 886	4 481
Total assets	**8 327**	**8 052**
Current liabilities		
Outstanding claims	1 423	1 415
Other	1 603	1 847
Total current liabilities	3 026	3 262
Non-current liabilities		
Outstanding claims	3 008	2 636
Statutory funds	831	864
Other	523	342
Total non-current liabilities	4 362	3 842
Total liabilities	**7 388**	**7 104**
Net assets	**939**	**946**
Outside equities	(12)	(11)
Shareholders' funds	927	935

a mere $18 million (according to its own accounts) net profit in 2000, which meant its stated $8.3 billion in total assets were generating almost nil return.

80 THE NUMBERS GAME

Another visible monster to someone who trawled the notes to accounts and understood insurance practice was the level of intangibles. In the current assets, for example, deferred acquisition costs totalled $304 million. These are the costs of acquiring policies. They represent money spent, but instead of being expensed against the profit and loss account for the year, up to 80 per cent of them have been capitalised. To take a tiny example, if a salesman spent $200 on travel, entertainment and other costs to sign up a client, only $40 of that might have been written off as an expense and the other $160 would be capitalised and written off over the duration of the policy. This accounting policy was not spelt out in the notes to HIH's accounts. One acid test of any asset is: 'What could this be sold for?' In the case of deferred acquisition costs, the answer would be close to zero.

Another $494 million intangibles can be seen under non-current assets. The notes revealed that $475 million of that amount was goodwill, mostly related to the takeover of FAI. Goodwill has been explained earlier, but broadly it represents the excess paid for a company over the fair value of the assets acquired. This goodwill was being amortised annually by HIH, but the $475 million still left on the books was a very large amount. Goodwill is justified on the grounds that the amount will be recouped through synergies and efficiencies of combining the raider and target companies. Alternatively, if the target company is generating profits for the raider, it can be treated as an asset. In the case of FAI, both these justifications were invalid because FAI had proved to be a bag of snakes for HIH. As mentioned above, the consolidated HIH group had made a net profit of a mere $18 million in 2000.

A third warning lurked in the notes related to the 'other' long-term assets. These included $228 million in future tax benefits available from recoupment of losses. As HIH had made such a small profit in 2000 (and a loss of $21 million the year before), the recoupment of these past tax losses looked most improbable.

Adding these numbers together ($304 million in deferred acquisition costs, $475 million goodwill and $228 million tax losses), we get a total of $1007 million in very soft assets. That more than wipes out the stated shareholders' funds of $927 million. This company is running on empty. Sell! Sell! Sell!

Those were the monsters which could be seen in the HIH accounts by an alert reader. In addition, there were others lurking unseen. Referring back to the 2000 balance sheet, the $3 billion estimate of outstanding liabilities was low. The biggest mistake of HIH was that the company notoriously always took an optimistic view of its outstanding liabilities, rather than a conservative one. Having made a central estimate, they never added a prudential margin. This was particularly dangerous policy because of the nature of the long-tail business already touched upon. The average gap between HIH writing a policy and paying a claim was two and a half to three years. Where claims are being paid anywhere up to 10 years or more after the premium has been collected, it becomes vitally important to take a prudent approach to estimates of future claims. HIH didn't.

Worse, if the money collected in premiums is inadequate to pay the resulting claims, an insurance company can mask that deficiency by growing the business. By selling more policies it has more premiums flowing in and that disguises the fact that the business is making losses.

This is exactly what happened with HIH, which became notorious for winning business by cutting premiums. It grew to eventually hold some 16 per cent of the Australian general insurance policy mainly by quoting rates that were below its competitors. Having sold policies at the wrong price, it masked the resulting losses by selling even more policies at the wrong prices, which multiplied the size of the ultimate—and, increasingly, inevitable—collapse. HIH was not an insurance company so much as a Ponzi scheme.

The balance sheet estimate of $3 billion in outstanding liabilities was low, but exactly how low will not be known until the final claims roll in. Hindsight estimates after it went bust estimated that its outstanding liabilities were low by around $400 million. Counsel assisting the Royal Commission reckoned HIH had underestimated its outstanding liabilities by $421 million. David Lombe of Deloitte, retained by the commission to make an expert opinion, put the figure in the range $383 to $503 million. The Royal Commissioner, Mr Justice Owen, learnedly guessed $302 million. The range of these guesses gives us an index of the difficulty that even honest and well-intentioned people encounter when trying to calculate an insurer's outstanding liabilities. But the most important point is that all the estimates were way above the $3 billion figure published in the HIH accounts. The company was badly under-provisioned (or under-reserved, it means the same thing) and there was almost no way any analyst could have told this from scrutinising HIH's published accounts.[7] Another invisible monster which no analyst could have uncovered was HIH's estimate of future claims handling costs. HIH reckoned the handling costs would be 2 per cent of the total. Industry experience was closer to 5 per cent. This would have added another $142 million to future liabilities.[8]

A third invisible monster was HIH's financial reinsurance contracts, some of which had been inherited from its disastrous takeover of FAI in 1998. During the Royal Commission, these contracts were referred to as 'sham' reinsurance contracts, which seems a fair description as their only practical purpose appears to have been to make the profit and loss account look better in the short term.

The worst of these contracts was one which FAI entered in 1998 with National Indemnity of the USA. National Indemnity provided cover for $50 million worth of claims over five years at a premium of $55 million. Manifestly, FAI was going to lose $5 million on the contract. However, it could book the recoveries at any time, so it booked $29 million of them in 1998, the first year of the contract. When offset against $5.5 million paid in premiums, that represented a 'profit' of $23.5 million to FAI. Quite obviously, however, there was still $49.5 million outstanding to be paid in premiums while only $21 million was left to be collected in recoveries. Therefore FAI was booking a $23.5 million profit for the first year, but was incurring an unrecognised loss of $28.5 million over the next four. To give this contract a faint appearance of risk, National Indemnity attached to this contract insurance cover of $30 million for earthquakes. However, to be collected Australia had to suffer two earthquakes, each causing losses in excess of $5 billion occurring in two of the five years. To put this in perspective, the most expensive earthquake in Australia's history until then had been at Newcastle in 1989 which had cost only $1.7 billion. That meant the earthquake 'risk' attached to FAI's contract was negligible. Even worse, the final National Indemnity contract was signed on 30 June of the first year (and if the evidence is examined carefully it may even have been signed after midnight), so the first of the five years had already passed. Sham reinsurance contracts such as these enabled FAI to pare its loss of $60 million in 1998 back to a few million dollars. The nature and effect of these reinsurance contracts was never disclosed in the accounts of FAI or of HIH and there was no way any analyst could have detected them. Outsiders knew nothing about these contracts until the Royal Commission uncovered them.

By June 2000, the non-existent assets being carried in HIH's accounts from such sham reinsurance contracts totalled $351 million. Again, there was no way any outside analyst could have detected this. Indeed, the unmasking of these sham contracts by the Royal Commission investigators was greeted with awe and disbelief.

Table 3.11 summarises Mr Justice Owen's estimates of the adjustments that should have been made to HIH's published 2000 accounts.

Table 3.11 Adjustments to HIH's 2000 balance sheet

Item	$m
Under-provisioning	283.4
FAI reinsurance recoveries	18.6
Future claims handling costs	142.0
Sham reinsurance contracts	351.1
Liability on converting notes	35.0
Deferred IT costs	8.6
Future income tax benefits	228.4
Goodwill	108.2
Total	1 175.3

Source: HIH Royal Commission[9]

Some of the numbers in Table 3.11 differ from those given in the text above, but don't worry about that. The real point is that HIH's $939 million stated shareholders' funds at 30 June 2000 would have been wiped out by these adjustments. Instead

84 THE NUMBERS GAME

of having nearly a billion in net assets, it was belly-up. And a similar series of adjustments to the 1999 accounts would have rendered it insolvent then too. So investors were left with the unsavoury prospect that an insurance company which had some 16 per cent of the Australian market had managed to produce accounts for two successive years showing it to be solvent when it wasn't. And those accounts had been signed off by one of the world's then top audit firms. There was actually a small note to the 2000 audit certificate saying that HIH used whole of account insurance contracts (these are the ones later referred to as shams), but the way the note was written gave no clue as to the extent of the underlying disaster.

When an insurer gets into the reinsurance market, its accounts become even more opaque because there is no way an outsider can know what sort of risks it has on its books. Every so often, for example, an Australian insurance company will disclose that it lost a few million on a hurricane in Florida.

This raises the question: What in Hades is an Australian insurer doing insuring hurricanes in Florida, where they happen regularly around September each year? The answer is that there are big premiums on the Florida hurricane business and if you score a year when there's no hurricane or where the hurricane doesn't hit your bit of Florida, you can make nice money. It's basically a bet on which way a wild wind is going to go.

But you can lose big too. In 1999 GIO Australia lost $130 million when the Gulf Coast of the USA was hit by Hurricane Georges. That seemed far too much for GIO (whose shareholders' funds were around a billion at the time) to be holding on one hurricane-prone area. It did not improve things that $50 million of the exposure was reinsurance and $80 million was retrocession. *Retrocession* is reinsurance of reinsurers, when the reinsurers want to lay off their bets. Retrocession insurance is low-premium (and on Gulf Coast hurricanes, high-risk). GIO got out of the retrocession business after that.

If an insurance company is inaccurately assessing its risks then sooner or later it is going to face a big payout. It may take years for the statistics to revert to the norm, but they will. The only way an insurer can flout the odds and survive is by luck, and sound insurance is about eliminating luck, not relying on it.

For all these reasons, insurance companies which hold inwards reinsurance business should make extra provisions for risk. This will vary depending on how well the insurer understands the business and its risks, but the rule of thumb in the industry is for the company to go tot up all the estimates outlined earlier for claims outstanding (the total is called the central estimate) and then add what is called a prudential margin of 20 per cent to its provisions. Some companies (including FAI and HIH at the time of writing) do not believe the prudential margin is necessary. This will enhance their profits, so keep this factor in mind when making comparisons between general insurance companies.

Modern insurance traces its origins to the London coffee houses where the Lloyds brokers used to operate in the seventeenth century. The City of London is still the world capital of the insurance business, and the broking houses there are steeped in centuries of experience. Among cynics in downtown Sydney there is a widely held theory that the lads in London keep all the good reinsurance business for themselves and farm the dud stuff out to dumb colonials on the other side of the world. Certainly GIO picked up some business that turned out horribly. GIO's losses between 1998 and 1999, including the need for replacement of capital, ultimately exceeded $1 billion.

How long is the tail? General insurance can be divided into two types of risk: long-tail and short-tail. Short-tail is business where claims are generally settled within a year, such as car accidents and house damage. Long-tail business is where claims are not settled within a year. Sometimes the insurer may not even know about long-tail claims for several years after the event has occurred; as in professional liability or asbestosis cases, for example.

Reinsurance business can contain a larger element of long-tail than is apparent from a superficial inspection. Let's say a London insurance company has reinsured the majority of its fire business and an Australian company has picked up 2 per cent of it. After a factory burns down in the Midlands, the head insurer in London refused to pay, claiming arson. The factory owner sues, the court case takes years and eventually the insurance

86 THE NUMBERS GAME

company loses. So five years after the fire, the London insurer sends the Australian insurer a notification that it has lost a $100 million case and will they please send a cheque for their share, that is, $2 million.

Worst of all, it might be more than 2 per cent. When the London company farmed out its fire business, there might have been 50 companies taking a piece of it. By the time the claim arrives, ten of them might have gone out of business (the mortality rate of small insurance companies around the world is rather alarming, especially in inwards reinsurance). So the liability of the Australian insurer has risen by one-quarter and it has to pay out $2.5 million.

These are the reasons why inward reinsurance from overseas was a graveyard for Australian companies in the 1990s. Australia's best-run insurance company in that time was probably QBE Insurance. QBE had a policy of refusing to accept inwards re-insurance unless it had a substantial enough presence in the country concerned to run its own checks on the business. It can be no coincidence that QBE was the company least scarred by reinsurance disasters in that decade.

Anyhow, if we combine all these factors, the most potentially dangerous kind of risk to hold is long-tail reinsurance bought from London by an Australian company with no overseas expertise.

PREJUDICE 14

The City of London didn't get rich by giving away profitable reinsurance business to Australians.

The question arises as to whether astute investors could have picked the looming disaster in GIO. The answer is that they could have. Consider the following segmental data taken from the GIO annual reports of 1996, 1997 and 1998 (Table 3.12). This table tells us quite a lot about the disaster. In 1996, GIO had an operating result of $202.1 million, of which slightly more than half ($105.5 million) was earned from inward reinsurance and corporate insurance. The return on revenue from the re-insurance business, at 14.4 per cent, was more than double that

Table 3.12 GIO segmental information

	Inward reinsurance $m	Other business $m	Total $m
Year to June 1996			
Operating result			
Australia	46.2	105.2	151.4
International	59.3	(8.6)	50.7
	105.5	96.6	202.1
Operating revenue			
Australia	204.3	1 372.1	1 576.4
International	527.0	15.8	542.8
	731.3	1 387.9	2 119.2
Total assets			
Australia	1 064.2	3 131.2	4 195.4
International	1 760.3	97.6	1 857.9
	2 824.5	3 228.8	6 053.3
Year to June 1997			
Operating result			
Australia	58.2	169.2	227.4
International	102.8	1.0	103.8
	161.0	170.2	331.2
Operating revenue			
Australia	313.8	1 499.9	1 813.7
International	785.1	34.6	819.7
	1 098.9	1 534.5	2 633.4
Operating assets			
Australia	1 178.2	3 321.0	4 499.2
International	2 021.2	111.0	2 132.2
	3 199.4	3 432.0	6 631.4
Year to June 1998			
Operating result			
Australia	(36.5)	82.4	45.9
International	(103.3)	2.2	(101.1)
	(139.8)	84.6	(55.2)
Operating revenue			
Australia	263.7	1 477.0	1 740.7
International	998.5	43.2	1 041.7
	1 262.2	1 520.2	2 782.4
Operating assets			
Australia	1 154.2	3 722.4	4 876.6
International	2 802.0	45.6	2 847.6
	3 956.2	3 768.0	7 724.2

88 THE NUMBERS GAME

on the rest of GIO's business, which earned only 7 per cent. In particular, the international business, with an operating result of $59.3 million, was earning a return of 11.3 per cent on revenue. Inward reinsurance and corporate insurance was also earning 3.7 per cent on total assets employed compared to 3 per cent for the rest of GIO's business. If you listen very hard, you can hear some GIO director saying: 'We're earning heaps more in overseas reinsurance than we are in boring old Australia. Why don't we go heavier into overseas reinsurance?'

So GIO did. If we look at the 1997 result, GIO upped its assets in inward reinsurance and corporate insurance by 13 per cent to $3.2 billion. Revenue in that category was up by 50 per cent to nearly $1.1 billion. The operating result showed a similar leap to $161 million. And as the numbers show, the big expansion was in the international business. The operating result of $161 million represented a return of 14.7 per cent on revenue, fractionally higher than in 1996. However, GIO's other business had also picked up. The profit there of $170.2 million represented a return on revenue of 11.1 per cent. And return on assets was 5 per cent for both reinsurance and other business.

It would not have been sensible to sell GIO at that point. The company was doing superbly, with an operating result up more than 60 per cent to $331 million. But the rapid expansion in overseas reinsurance would have worried an experienced investor. The number of Australian companies which have prospered in overseas reinsurance is close to zero and GIO was really stepping up its exposure in the area.

GIO continued its expansion in inward reinsurance and corporate insurance in 1998. Assets employed in these classes of business had risen to comprise 51 per cent of all GIO's assets, from 48 per cent in the previous year. Assets employed in the international business rose to $2.8 billion—38 per cent up on the previous year and nearly 60 per cent higher than in 1996. Revenue from the international business had not risen as quickly, being up by only 27 per cent over 1997.

So, GIO was writing more business overseas for lower revenue. And the result had been a black eye. GIO had lost $103 million on its international reinsurance business and a further $36.5 million domestically. The accounts containing this data were released in mid-October of 1998. To remind readers of the chronology, GIO announced on 17 August that it had suffered a shock loss in re-insurance during the June half of 1998. AMP Ltd bid for GIO on 25 August. In December, AMP lifted its bid to $5.35 a share. Throughout the bid, GIO directors declared the AMP bid to be inadequate. A shareholder studying the above data, however, could easily have decided (as the majority of them did) that maybe GIO wasn't doing too well in its expansion into reinsurance and so maybe they should accept the bid after all.

PREJUDICE 15

Before getting carried away by hype, particularly in a takeover battle, just check the numbers.

If all this analysis on insurance companies sounds like hard work, that's because it is. Any investor who puts money into insurance stocks without doing all this dreary analysis will sooner or later be at the mercy of smarter investors who have done the hard yards. Insurance companies have an image of solidity which can be quite misleading, as GIO and Reinsurance Australia have demonstrated. If you haven't the skill or inclination to do the heavy analysis, find someone who can (a retired actuary would be pretty good) or leave insurance stocks alone.

Banks

The only thing worth knowing about a bank is whether a sub-stantial proportion of its borrowers are liable to default. Until recently, there was no reliable way of predicting this from a bank's published accounts, so investors could have saved them-selves a great deal of time by not reading them. They're a bit more informative these days, however.

One point worth bearing in mind whenever reading the accounts of a bank—or any other financial institution—is that their stock in trade is money. To all other kinds of company, money is a means of payment and a yardstick of valuation. In a

90 THE NUMBERS GAME

bank, money is what the company buys and sells, just like a jam company sells jars of marmalade.

The price of money is the interest rate and—to the extent that a bank is dealing in foreign currencies—the exchange rate. To really assess a bank therefore, it is necessary to look very closely at the nature of the risks it may be exposed to if there is a change in either of those prices. This will take us into some of the most arcane areas of any balance sheet, so perhaps we'd better start with relatively simple analysis.

Profit and loss accounts

Let's begin with the 1999 accounts of Westpac Banking Corporation, one of Australia's big four banks.

The profit and loss statement for the year to 30 September— with the tax gross-up stripped out to avoid confusing the innocent[10]—looked like Table 3.13.

Table 3.13 Westpac profit and loss, 30 September 1999

	$m
Interest income	8 348
Interest expense	(4 856)
Net interest income	3 492
Non-interest income	2 139
Total operating income	5 631
Bad and doubtful debt charge	(171)
Non-interest expenses	(3 434)
Profit before tax	2 026
Income tax	(567)
Net profit	1 459
Minorities	(3)
Profit attributable to shareholders	1 456

So Westpac made a profit of more than $1.4 billion for 1998–99. Was that good or bad? Well, considering that former chief executive Stuart Fowler went to his grave before achieving his objective of a billion dollar profit—good. It just took a few more years than he hoped.

What are the important numbers for a bank? Well, the ratio

of interest income to interest expense is important. A bank exists by borrowing money from depositors at one rate and lending it to clients at a higher rate. If it can't make a margin on that, it's out of business. So divide the second line in the P&L account into the first and it tells you that Westpac earned $1.72 interest for every $1 it paid during the year. Good. That's quite a nice margin.

Note that some 20 per cent of Westpac's total revenue was derived from non-interest income. This would include fees (for fund management, underwriting, loan arranging etc.), profits on investments and the like. These items have become a more substantial proportion of Westpac's total income in recent times. To measure the bank's efficiency we should look at return on revenue.

Total revenue is interest income plus non-interest income, which is $10 487 million. Divide that into the pre-tax profit ($2026m ÷ $10 487m) and we find that out of every $100 income for Westpac that year, $19.31 went to the bottom line. Excellent. Very good margin.

How was its return on assets? Let's look at a very abbreviated balance sheet (Table 3.14).

Table 3.14 Westpac balance sheet, 30 September 1999

	$m
Assets	
Loans	97 716[a]
Other assets	42 504
Total assets	**140 220**
Liabilities	
Liabilities	128 531
Loan capital	2 692
Total liabilities	**131 223**
Shareholders' funds	**8 997**

Note: [a]After deducting $1500m in bad debt provisions

Shareholders' funds of nearly $9 billion represented only 6.4 per cent of total assets—quite low compared with the roughly

50 per cent ratio expected in an industrial company. To shareholders' funds can be added the loan capital. These are subordinated loans which rank behind the other liabilities of the bank such as its debts to depositors. Loan capital and shareholders' funds together total $11 689 million, representing 8.4 per cent of total assets.

Australian banks are required by law to maintain a capital asset ratio. In 1999, Westpac's Tier 1 capital (basically shareholders' funds as a ratio of total assets) was 7 per cent, well above the statutory minimum of 4 per cent. Its Tier 1 and 2 capital, which includes loan capital, totalled 9.2 per cent, compared to the statutory minimum of 8 per cent. These are quite comfortable margins. The Tier 1 and 2 ratios are calculated by adjusting various assets for risk. The lay reader is spared having to make the calculations on capital adequacy,[11] but—as we see from the above example—a ballpark figure can usually be reached by a simple calculation of the ratios of shareholders' funds and loan capital to total assets. The Tier 1 and 2 ratios are imposed to ensure that banks are maintaining adequate capital to meet their obligations in an emergency.

Note that banks do not need as high a percentage of shareholders' funds to equity as industrial companies. Because they deal in money they should be more liquid. That is, if a depositor wants to withdraw money, a bank should be able to cash in its short-term assets to the same extent and stay liquid. That's the theory, and in all normal times it is so. In practice, some of the most exciting and dramatic times in Australia's financial history (and the world's) have occurred when that didn't happen. In truth, if all the depositors turned up on the doorstep one morning and demanded their money back, there probably isn't a bank in the world that could pay them all. That is because while banks hold most of their deposits at call, most of their assets are invested for terms of anywhere from one month to 25 years. Even though overdrafts are technically repayable at call, it would engender chaos to seek to recall the lot. That is why assessment of liquidity is so important in analysing a bank. The banking system is built on the premise that all the depositors will never arrive on the same day. The banking system therefore depends very heavily on the degree of confidence that depositors have in their institution. When they lose that confidence, as they did in the 1890s, the consequences are frightening.

In Westpac's case the liabilities of $128.5 billion included some $85.5 billion of deposits and public borrowings. On the other side, the deposits included $97 billion in loans to customers. The loans may be perfectly sound, in that the customers will repay them over time, but obviously they could not all be collected overnight.

Ratios

A few more calculations. If we take Westpac's 1999 loan figure of $97 716 million and add back the bad debt provisions of $1500 million (Table 3.14), total loans were $99 216 million. The bad debt provisions of $1500 million represent 1.51 per cent of that figure. So Westpac reckons that for every $100 it has loaned, $1.51 might not be recovered. Comfortably low. During the 1999 financial year, the profit and loss account (Table 3.13) shows the net increase in bad debt provisions was a mere $171 million. As a proportion of total year-end loans outstanding that is only 0.17 per cent. Very low indeed. Return on assets (pre-tax profit to total assets) is 1.44 per cent—not terrific by any other company's standards but okay for a bank. When looking at a bank's return on assets (ROA, as it's often termed), it is always worth keeping in mind the earnings per share figure. In Westpac's case in 1999 that was 77 cents a share. That's the number investors tend to focus on, and in Westpac's case it was fairly comforting in 1999.

Now let's go back in time and compare Westpac's 1999 key numbers with those of 1988 (Table 3.15).

How did the bank's shape and performance compare? Interest income was not much bigger in 1999 that it was in 1988—a reflection of the much lower interest rates prevailing at the end of the twentieth century. Interest expense had been pruned and the ratio between interest income and expense (which was pretty good in 1988) had become even stronger. Pre-tax profit had risen sharply in 1999, both in the absolute number and as a percentage of total income. Total assets had grown strongly but ROA was steady at 1.44 per cent. Bad debt provisions had grown in 1999

94 THE NUMBERS GAME

Table 3.15 Key Westpac numbers and ratios

	1988	1999
Interest income	$8 174m	$8 348m
Interest expense	$5 555m	$4 856m
Interest income/expense (times)	1.47	1.74
Pre-tax profit	$1 225m	$2 026m
Total income	$9 447m	$10 316m
Pre-tax profit/total income	13.0%	19.6%
Total assets	$84 579m	$140 220m
Pre-tax profit/total assets	1.45%	1.44%
Loans to customers[a]	$48 068m	$99 216m
Bad debt provisions	$660m	$1 500m
Bad debts/loans	1.37%	1.51%
Shareholders' funds	$5 499m	$8 997m
Sh. funds + loan capital	$7 590m	$11 689m
Sh. funds/total assets	6.5%	6.4%
Sh. funds + loan capital/total assets	9.0%	8.9%
Capital asset ratio	9.4%	9.2%

Note: [a]Before bad debt provisions

both in dollar terms and as a proportion of total loans outstanding. But at 1.51 per cent in 1999, bad loans were still a tolerably small proportion of the loan book. If the numbers were all we had to go by, it would be fair to conclude that Westpac's lending was slightly more adventurous in 1999 than it was in 1988. Shareholders' funds had grown and so had loan capital, but the bank's gearing had hardly changed, expressed as equity, loan capital or both as a percentage of total assets. Indeed, the 1988 bank looked slightly sounder as measured by its capital asset ratio.

All of which proves that we have been wasting our time. In 1988 Westpac was on the threshold of a near-death experience, but there was absolutely no way that could have been foretold just by reading the numbers in its accounts. Almost before the ink was dry on the 1988 accounts Westpac began discovering huge bad debts made to corporate cowboys of the day, such as George Herscu's Hooker Corporation and Abe Goldberg's Linter Group. Huge losses were unveiled in subsidiaries such as Australian Guarantee Corporation, where there were enormous property exposures, and Bill Acceptance Corporation. More than $200 million had been spent on a computer project called CS90 which never worked. Another subsidiary called Partnership Pacific became embroiled in scandal when many of its clients lost money on foreign currency exposures.

Between 1989 and 1993 Westpac would write-off more than $6.3 billion. A rights issue of $1.2 billion was required in 1992 to maintain Westpac's capital. The market panicked at Westpac's seemingly endless announcements of large losses and the share price crashed below the $3 rights issue price. A shortfall of a staggering $883 million had to be picked up by the underwriters, CS First Boston. Until then, it had been unthinkable that an issue by Australia's oldest, proudest bank could possibly have a shortfall.[12] If it had not been for the CS First Boston underwriting, the issue might have failed in which case Westpac could have been in breach of its capital adequacy requirements. This would have created a first-class crisis both in the bank and the Australian banking system. Luckily, it never happened.

None of this potential disaster was even faintly discernible from the 1988 accounts, which were unqualified by the auditors. Indeed, the then chairman of Westpac, Sir James Foots, in the opening statement of that annual report, announced a profit increase of 69 per cent for 1987–88 and declared this to be 'a splendid performance' by the bank.

For many years afterwards the board and management of Westpac blamed each other for the bank's ghastly performance. This book is not about attributing blame: it is about trying to understand company accounts. And on the evidence of Westpac in 1988, it is clear that if the board and management don't understand what a bank is doing, the investor has no hope of comprehending it from the group accounts. In small companies, there can be clues which the lay investor or the acute analyst may pick up from the balance sheet and profit and loss account. When big companies get their accounts wrong, the first clues usually emerge in the share market. It never ceases to amaze how often the market reflects defects in a company which the analysts and rating companies only discover later.

96 THE NUMBERS GAME

PREJUDICE 16

Banks are so large that you can hide a mammoth in their accounts.

There must have been several hidden in the Westpac 1988 accounts. To be fair, by 1999 the banks had greatly improved their standards of reporting. The financial section of the Westpac 1999 annual report gives some detail on credit standards and bad loans, although the reader has to hunt through the notes to find them.

There's a table on credit quality analysis, which gives the provision for bad and doubtful debts ($1.5 billion), ratios of bad debts to total loans (1.51 per cent) and the total write-offs for the year. Westpac also gives comparative figures over three years, which show the total of bad debts to be declining. The bank also spends some seven pages of its report discussing risk management and the various types of risk exposure—credit risk, market risk and operational risk. All very good. A bank that discloses that much information can't have much to hide.

One figure always worth checking in the accounts of any lending institution is the level of *non-accrual loans*. A non-accrual loan is one upon which a bank has stopped accruing interest and against which specific provisions have been made for loss. The term is also used to describe loans where security is insufficient to cover the amount owing.

The first point about a non-accrual loan is that the bank should be aware of it. If a customer can't pay interest on a loan any more then it has become a non-accrual loan. It's a little more difficult to define a non-accrual loan where a customer such as a property developer has been accruing interest on a construction loan and has agreed to repay the interest as soon as the property starts selling. However, a bank with good management should recognise early when a property development is becoming uneconomic. The trouble with Westpac in 1988 was that heaps of developers became basket cases before the bank realised anything untoward was happening.

Westpac's reporting is now considerably more comprehensive. Note 13 to the 1999 accounts not only gives the details of non-accrual loans, but also comparative figures for the previous four years (Table 3.16).

Table 3.16 Westpac's non-accruals

| | All figures in $m | | | | |
	1999	1998	1997	1996	1995
Non-accrual loans	619	784	783	1 261	2 081
Restructured loans	25	68	86	92	115
Provisions	(330)	(362)	(339)	(531)	(950)
Net impaired assets	314	490	530	822	1 246
Impaired assets/loans	0.60%	0.83%	0.94%	1.56%	2.88%

Comforting. Not only have non-accrual and restructured loans fallen in absolute terms, but they are also down as a percentage of average loans and acceptances.

The calculation of interest rate margins, return on revenue and the rest mentioned earlier will tell an analyst how a bank is performing. The more basic question to answer is whether it is capable of surviving in tough times, such as the recession of 1990–92.

One little test is to see whether the bank has free capital. This can be gauged by adding up the money tied up by a bank in fixed assets and investments then subtracting that sum from shareholders' funds (Table 3.17).

Table 3.17 Westpac's free capital, parent company accounts

		1999 $m		1988 $m
Shareholders' funds		8 994		5 434
Less				
Fixed assets	1 527		1 032	
Investments in controlled entities	6 595		6 835	
Other investments	780		166	
		8 902		8 033
Free capital		92		(2 599)

98 THE NUMBERS GAME

Well, in 1999 Westpac did have free capital that it could use to cover bad loans or risk assets in their portfolio. It didn't have much, but it was in a far healthier state than it had been in 1988. Table 3.17 gives one of the clues why Westpac was so vulnerable at that time.

It is also worth checking the deposit structure. As has been mentioned earlier, banks sometimes have to endure panics. Let's say a bank has borrowed money from depositors at call and has loaned the money to home owners to finance their house purchases. If a large proportion of depositors rush in and demand their money back, the bank will have difficulty liquidating the mortgages which might all be for 25 years. This inspired the hackneyed saying that 'banks should lend short and borrow long'. But in practice that is rarely feasible. Usually a bank cannot avoid having large amounts in call deposits such as cheque accounts and its best earning assets are often loans to businesses and home owners which would not be easily liquidated. So banks customarily borrow short and lend long. But they should make some effort to push out the maturity of their deposits. It is equally important that they should make some effort to spread their deposits. It is far safer to have call deposits spread across half a million individuals rather than rely on a handful of large institutional investors who could withdraw at any time.

Banks now give considerably more detail on these spreads, as is shown in Table 3.18, drawn from Note 32 to the Westpac 1999 accounts. This note showed interest rate risk, because sensitivity to interest rates arises from mismatches in the rates being earned by loans and the corresponding rates being paid on the deposits which fund them.

The original table included off-balance-sheet items and foreign assets and liabilities which have been omitted. Just looking at this very simplified tabulation, the mismatches appear tolerable. Westpac actually had more assets at call (such as short-dated bank and government bills) than it had liabilities. There was a mismatch in the opposite direction in the one-to-three month maturities, but not a large one in the overall context of Westpac.

A final point worth checking is the overall balance of a bank's business. In the late 1980s several Australian banks lurched into

Table 3.18 Westpac interest rate risk, 1999

Total $m	Less than 1 month $m	1 to 3 months $m	3 to 12 months $m	1 to 5 years $m	5+ years $m	Non-interest bearing $m
Australia						
Assets 110 554	60 590	7 706	6 397	11 736	619	23 506
Liabilities 104 012	59 045	15 586	2 771	232	348	26 030

trouble because they were too heavily exposed to the corporate cowboys of the day and to property. In those years banks' public accounts gave few clues on the spread of their business. That has now changed. Notes to bank accounts now routinely show how their loans are spread between different categories of customers (government, agriculture, commercial etc.). The notes also show the spread of maturities for each category (one year, five years, and so on). In Westpac's case the spreads are shown over a five-year history, giving a reader of the balance sheet an instant grasp of how well the loan portfolio is distributed and where the movements have been.

Derivative exposures

It was mentioned earlier that as a bank's stock in trade is money, its risks are associated with movements in the price of money— either by changes to interest rates or currency rates. We dealt above with the interest rate exposure. Currency exposure is—or should be—handled through the use of derivatives. This leads to an examination of the most complex item to be found in any set of accounts—a bank's derivative exposure.

Being financial intermediaries, banks are always bound to have some degree of exposure to derivatives markets. They have to settle foreign exchange debts and exposures on behalf of their customers. The two most common forms of derivative transactions for banks are foreign exchange forwards and interest rate swaps.

100 THE NUMBERS GAME

How does a forex forward work? An import company orders goods, knowing it will be liable to pay US$1 million in a year's time for them. Let us say the prevailing exchange rate is A$0.60 to the US$. At that rate, the Australian importer will have to pay A$1 666 667 when the bill falls due in twelve months. Having lodged its order, the importer faces a currency risk. If the A$ should be weaker against the US$ in twelve months, the importer will have to pay a higher sum. So through a bank, the importer buys US$1 million twelve months forward. (It might actually be a sounder practice to buy only US$500 000, which would put the importer in a median position between the A$ and US$ but let's stick to the full US$1 million for the sake of the example.)

To buy forward, the importer may have to pay a premium of, say, 140 basis points—a basis point being one-hundredth of a cent. The calculation then becomes US$1 million divided by 0.586 (A$0.60 minus 140 basis points), which equals A$1 706 485. The real benefit is that by locking in the price of the goods, the importer has fixed one of its most important business costs, and that should enable more efficient planning.

Which leads us to the derivative position of the bank. Westpac's in 1999 is shown in Table 3.19 (truncated from the original).

Yes, the table makes me feel the same way you do. It gives one a great urge to go and lie down quietly and hope the numbers will somehow disappear. But let's work through a few anyway.

The total figure for interest rate and forex derivatives is $485 billion, which would alarm any lay reader who didn't understand the numbers. After all, $485 billion was more than three times Westpac's total assets at the same date (see Table 3.14) and 54 times its net assets. What is the bank doing horsing around with all these derivatives?

The answer is that a lot, if not all, of the derivatives should belong to the customers. Looking first at the forex derivatives, if our importer above had bought the forward foreign exchange cover through Westpac, $1 706 485 of this exposure would have been his. This immediately shows why we should not be too alarmed at the notional amounts shown in the table, because

Table 3.19 Westpac trading derivatives outstanding, 30 September 1999

	Notional amount $m	Regulatory credit equivalent $m	Positive mark-to-market (replacement cost) $m
Interest rate			
Futures	29 148	—	—
Forwards	32 828	6	6
Swaps	140 350	2 485	1 837
Purchased options	15 833	17	11
Sold options	3 941	8	—
Foreign exchange			
Forwards	211 665	4 753	2 356
Swaps	25 915	1 892	737
Purchased options	11 464	535	330
Sold options	12 206	—	—
Commodities	1 099	149	39
Equities	723	63	13
Total	**485 222**	**9 908**	**5 329**

whatever happens our importer's US$1 million is not going to be worthless. No cash has yet changed hands in that transaction. The currencies can move in either direction. By settlement day the A$ might be worth either US$0.55 or US$0.65. Table 3.20 shows the resulting A$ equivalents for US$1 million and the importer's gain forgone or loss averted.

One risk that the bank is taking is that the importer will honour the obligation to buy the US$1 million. Let us say that on settlement day the A$ is worth US$0.65 and the importer reneges, either because the importer has gone broke or decided to buy US dollars spot. In practice the bank could sue him, but in the short term, being committed to buy the US$1 million, the bank has to cover and is out of pocket by $168 023. This will be its loss on the contract unless it manages to recover anything from the importer.

Table 3.20 Importer's gains or losses

US$	Exchange rate	A$	A$ gain/(loss)
1 000 000	.586	1 706 485	—
1 000 000	.65	1 538 461	168 023
1 000 000	.55	1 818 182	(111 697)

The bank monitors (or should monitor) this situation daily. On each day the transaction is marked-to-market so that the bank knows what the cost would be if it had to replace the contract. This is why the third column in Table 3.19 (the derivatives table) is headed 'replacement cost'. That column represents the real exposure of Westpac. In the example we have been working through, our importer would account for $168 023 of the $5.3 billion if the A$ had gone to US$0.65.

Broadly, if all Westpac's customers had defaulted on derivative obligations on 30 September 1999, Westpac would have been out of pocket by $5.3 billion less what it could retrieve by suing their socks off. Of course, this is quite an unrealistic scenario. And while we're still talking large money—$5.3 billion being 60 per cent of Westpac's net assets—obviously the threat is not as dire as the notional total would make it appear.

The second column shows the credit equivalents of the derivatives. This represents the Reserve Bank of Australia (RBA) putting its foot down. For many years the Australian banks' derivatives positions were not shown on their balance sheets. This bothered the RBA, which believed that as banks had to hold capital against the risks that they took on ordinary loans, they should also hold capital against any risks they took on derivatives. For currency forwards of less than one year, the RBA laid down a guideline that the capital adequacy requirement should be replacement cost plus 1 per cent of face value. Assuming once again that the A$ had risen from US$0.60 to US$0.65, the credit equivalent on our hypothetical importer's hypothetical default would be found by the following calculation:

Calculating credit equivalent

Replacement cost	$168 023
1 per cent of face value ($1 706 485)	$17 065
Credit equivalent	$185 088

The amount of capital which the bank needs to hold against this exposure is found by the following formula:

Credit equivalent $\times$ counter-party weighting = risk adjusted assets
Risk adjusted assets $\times$ 0.08 = capital adequacy requirement

The counter-party weighting is, roughly, the credit rating of the counter-party on the other side of the transaction, who is selling the US dollars to the bank. If the counter-party is a government agency the weighting is 0 per cent, which means the bank needs to provide no capital. If it is an OECD bank the weighting is 20 per cent and if it is a corporate the weighting is 100 per cent. In practice banks should do their own weightings and calculations, which ought to be more sophisticated.

Swaps

Along with foreign forward exchange contracts, the main type of derivative deal done by Australian banks is the interest rate swap. A swap is typically an exchange of a floating interest rate obligation for a fixed rate, or vice versa. A company might borrow money from a bank on a bill line where the interest rate is adjusted quarterly to keep pace with the market. The company decides it would prefer a fixed rate, so the bank does a swap with a counter-party.

For example, let's say Company A has borrowed $10 million from Bank B for three years at a current bank bill rate of 7.5 per cent. But the company fears that interest rates are going to rise and wants to fix its liability, so Bank B then does a swap with Bank C for a fixed rate of 9 per cent. The banks themselves tend to be big players in this market for the excellent reason that swaps enable them to at least partially escape the classic trap of borrowing short and lending long.

The overwhelming majority of Bank B's liabilities are to depositors who receive a floating rate of interest. Some of Bank B's assets are mortgages set at a fixed rate of interest. Apart from the swaps it does on behalf of Company A, Bank B will have a strong motive to swap its fixed interest mortgage portfolio for floating interest receipts so that it has at least a partial match between the rates on its liabilities and assets. Frequently Bank B will have to go offshore to find a counter-party. If that is the case, the interest rate swap will be accompanied by a swap of currency risks as well.

When a bank is acting as a principal in a derivative transaction, rather than as an agent on behalf of a customer, the bank is called the 'end user'. Australian banks now show end-user activity in their annual reports. In Westpac's case in September 1999, the total notional amount of $485 billion included $99 billion of internal transactions. Of that about $25 billion was in forex and the rest in interest rate swaps and options. Again, nowhere near the whole $99 billion would be at risk.

Taking a broader view of derivatives, there are three areas of risk for a bank. The first is the risk of inadequate credit assessment of customers and counter-parties. This is not peculiar to the modern derivatives market. Proper credit assessment has always been integral to banking throughout history. The history of banking failures is the history of banks with bad credit control. We saw some vivid examples in the late 1980s and early 1990s.

The second risk is market risk. Derivatives are volatile. Any bank that has poorly structured management or computer systems, or sloppy procedures, can quickly get into trouble—like a surfer caught by a rip.

The third risk is operational. If a rogue derivatives manager can run wild, as Nick Leeson did in Baring's Singapore office, that one manager can bring down a whole bank.

Working through the numbers, as we have in this exercise, should provide some degree of comfort to anyone who has invested in bank shares. Disclosure has been improved and investor safety is greater, but it's still worth running a check on banks' numbers. They behaved so foolishly in the 1980s it's difficult to believe they have entirely learned their lessons.

Mining companies

Very simply, mining is about earthmoving. A mining company digs up dirt which contains a valuable element. It extracts the valuable element, sells it and somehow gets rid of the dirt from which it cannot extract value. The valuable bit that is sold has to cover the cost of extraction and processing plus overheads such as depreciation and administration.

Now let's introduce a few complications.

Does the valuable bit exist?

Sometimes it doesn't. The mine may have been salted. The biggest and most famous salting in history happened to a deposit named Busang in the middle of Kalimantan. Busang contained traces of gold, but not enough to be payable. Rights to the deposit were then bought by a small Canadian stock called Bre-X Minerals which started reporting a massive gold deposit.

Over two years the estimated reserves at Busang rose from two million ounces to 30 million. Finally Bre-X was claiming reserves of 70 million ounces and its exploration chief, Dr John Felderhof, was claiming it could contain 200 million ounces. Even at 70 million it was easily the biggest gold deposit in the world. Then check assays early in 1997 showed all the reporting to be fraudulent. The assays had been tampered with systematically for two years.

The Bre-X share price collapsed, investors were wiped out and a scandal reverberated around the world. Michael de Guzman, the geologist who had been in charge of the Busang work, allegedly died after falling from a helicopter. A search found a body in the jungle, but it had been partly eaten by wild animals and such was the suspicion aroused by Bre-X by this time that there were suggestions that it might have been someone else. Nobody was ever convicted of salting, or even charged, which is enough reason for investors who value their peace of mind to avoid mining ventures in Canada and Indonesia for life.

Very few professionals guessed that Busang might have been salted until late in the piece. The sheer scale of the salting operation was mind-boggling. The world has never seen salting on that scale before and probably never will again. Usually a salting is a quick hit by some prospectors who juice up a few samples in an effort to sell some doggy mining prospect. The spectacle of methodical salting involving dozens of workers over two years was amazing. There were clues, however. One was that other

106 THE NUMBERS GAME

mining companies had scratched around the same area and found only sub-economic gold. This was not a strong clue, because it is not uncommon in mining for a company to walk away from a deposit that subsequently proves valuable. Mining history is littered with such incidents. A better clue was the purported size of Busang. The salting was so enthusiastic that Busang was being reported as the world's biggest gold mine, far larger than anything else ever known in modern mining. Okay, Busang was in a remote part of the world which had only been lightly explored, but it was equivalent to finding a twenty-foot man living in the Borneo jungle. The size of Busang was out of whack with mines anywhere in the world and out of whack with the closest ones in Kalimantan.

From time to time the market goes wild when a prospector or a company hits a spectacularly rich block of mineralisation. Sometimes it's a genuine find, but often it is a freakish small patch or a salting. It normally pays to be a little wary of such hot finds.

PREJUDICE 17

Incredible mineral finds usually stay incredible.

Exploration

The first step for a mining company is to find something worth digging up, so it goes exploring. Exploration, for all the glamour of the word, usually starts off in a mundane fashion.

Quite a lot of exploration occurs in the dusty files of the local Department of Mines. Australia has a rich mining history stretching back two centuries and much of what was found—or thought to be found—has been recorded. Ploughing through records of old mining fields can yield a lot of information and give pointers to the future.

Exploration in the field can cover a wide range of technologies, including geochemical sampling, geological mapping, seismic surveys and aeromagnetic surveys. Normally drill rigs—the ultimate symbol of exploration—are only brought on site after a company is satisfied that it has a worthwhile target.

By definition, exploration is costly and uncertain. One study in 1984 found that between 1955 and 1978 a total of $1618 million had been spent on mining exploration in Australia (excluding oil and gas).[13] Thousands of mineral occurrences had been discovered but only about 43 were thought to be economic with even fewer being actually developed. At best, this represents an average exploration cost of $38 million per deposit. Very few mines indeed could justify exploration costs of that dimension, so the conclusion must be that most exploration dollars were spent without finding a viable deposit. To put it another way, any exploration company that starts up with $5 or $10 million will have to be very lucky, or very clever, or both to strike a payable mine.

Of course, exploration techniques have improved considerably since 1978 and today's explorers have a better chance of finding an orebody (with the important proviso that they are honestly run). In practice what happens is that small exploration companies stay alive by farming out interests in their ground to other companies. Exploration remains high reward but also high risk. Most exploration companies never find a paying mine and even fewer pay a dividend.

Speculators in exploration stocks would do well to follow companies whose directors have previously found at least one paying mine. It also helps if the directors have a reputation for honesty. Many a mining company has raised millions from investors, then spent the lot buying worthless ground from the directors.

Interpreting drillholes

In a properly conducted exploration program, the drill rig appears late on the scene. First there will have been consultation of old mining records, soil sampling, aeromagnetic surveys and a host of less glamorous preliminary work aimed at identifying a promising area as a target for drilling. Only then will the exploration company commit to the expense of hiring drill rigs.

When Western Mining hit its historic three metres of 8.3 per cent nickel at Kambalda in 1966, the exploration team was ecstatic. That single drill intersection was long enough and

108 THE NUMBERS GAME

rich enough to tell them they were standing on a mine. It was a happy but very rare success. More typically a drilling program will take dozens or even hundreds of holes to painstakingly build up a picture of the potential orebody below the ground.

Eight per cent nickel or one ounce gold are good discoveries anywhere and any time, but the typical program deals in far lower grades. What constitutes a good drillhole will depend upon the mineral being sought and its price. And as the prices of all minerals will vary widely over time, it is not possible to lay down any hard and fast numbers here as to what constitutes an economic grade. After all, if the gold price slumps from A$500 to A$400 an ounce, any gold discovered in the next drillhole will be 20 per cent less valuable and the break-even grade might rise from, say, 2 grams per tonne to 2.5 grams.

Also, what constitutes a viable grade will depend upon the nature of the mineral. Coal mines typically comprise continuous seams several feet thick. Precious and base metal orebodies come in an infinite variety of shapes and may be patchy. Viability also depends on the nature of the mineral occurrence. An assay of one ounce of gold per tonne may not be viable if it is a small, isolated intersection deep underground or if it is associated with minerals such as antimony which will make the gold difficult to separate. On the other hand, an average grade of one gram may be viable if there is a lot of it close to the surface and it can be easily milled. During the early 1990s it was possible to retrieve gold economically from old tailings at grades below one gram.

Two figures worth remembering in gold exploration are that 31 grams equate to an ounce and one gram per tonne equates to one part per million. It does not take Einstein to work out that the lower the grade, the more necessary it will be to recover as much of the gold as possible. As a very rough rule of thumb, work on the principle that the effective grade will be reduced by between 5 and 10 per cent when actual mining starts. Some gold will be left in the ground because it is inaccessible or just plain missed. Some will not be recovered in the treatment circuit and will go through to tailings. A company which is recovering more than 95 per cent of gold is highly efficient. A company recovering less than 85 per cent is a worry unless it has a good excuse.

In this respect, watch for the word 'refractory'. It's a danger signal because it means that for some reason the ore will be difficult to treat. In refractory ores, gold recovery may be anywhere from 85 per cent down to 65 per cent. So if the in situ ore grade is 10 grams per tonne, the company might only recover 6.5 grams.

This is all worth bearing in mind when studying drill results. The first point to consider is whether the company has disclosed all its drilling results or just a few holes. In the early stages of exploration where a lot of wildcats are drilled, there will be plenty of holes that come up with nothing. These have a certain negative value because they tell the company where the orebody isn't, but there's not much point in releasing their results. So after a quarter of drilling, the company may release the results of only half a dozen holes, which will invariably be its best ones.

An investor has little chance of making sense of these results if they are not accompanied by some detail. Grid locations (1200 north, 500 west and so on) will give the relationship of the holes to each other. The closer they are the more accurate a picture can be drawn of what they have discovered. But the grid location only shows the point where the drill entered the ground. They are normally drilled at an angle of about 60 degrees, so the company also needs to disclose which way the drill was pointing. Otherwise four separate drillholes—north, south, east and west—could all have drilled through the same spot in the centre.

It also pays to be aware that drill intersections are quoted in averages. When a company says it struck an intersection of three metres averaging 3 grams per tonne, that could mean one metre of 0.9 grams, one of 1.1 grams and one of 7 grams. Also be aware that the three main drilling methods vary in accuracy. Diamond drills are the most precise but because of their expense are not much used in preliminary exploration. Reverse circulation (RC) drilling is less accurate because of the way the core is recovered and rotary air blast (RAB) is less accurate still. Nevertheless, even a RAB drill recovering three grams over three metres is indicating that there's gold down there somewhere around that level.

110 THE NUMBERS GAME

PREJUDICE 18

Don't worry about the grades so much; worry about the time the exploration program is taking. And worry if last year's hot exploration prospect no longer rates No. 1 mention in the quarterly report.

If a company is on to something it believes is a hot discovery, it should be giving the prospect priority and exploring it vigorously. If the deposit is any good it should be reflected in the drill results. A year's intensive exploration—two years at the outside— should be enough to establish whether the deposit is viable. Companies which muck around with a prospect for longer than that have usually run out of either cash or good drilling results. Many a company has announced a hot drilling result that sparked a boost for its shares, and then gone strangely quiet. It's invariably a sign there's something wrong.

Resources and reserves

Assuming the company is well run and lucky, it might strike valuable minerals. Our company will then issue a statement about its estimated resource or reserve.

Those two words sound disarmingly similar, but the difference between them can be as big as the Grand Canyon. It can be the difference between a bonanza and a duster. Without going into the fine print of the jargon, a *resource* is a chunk of mineralised ground, while a *reserve* is that part of the resource which on best available estimates looks like it can be mined at a profit. Putting it another way, a reserve should be profitable but a resource won't be profitable until it becomes a reserve. There are heaps of resources around Australia containing interesting grades of gold, silver, uranium, zinc, tantalum and so forth that have never become reserves because it has never been economical to mine them.

Any one of a number of factors can stop a resource from becoming a reserve. The most usual one is that the grade is too low. Another is that the resource is covered by too much overburden, so that the cost of moving all the surface dirt will make the resource too expensive to mine. Another is that the metallurgy is too difficult. The metal may be too fine-grained or it may be combined with other substances that will make it too expensive to separate. Resources and reserves come in categories. Working from the bottom up, resources can be inferred, indicated or measured, and reserves can be probable or proven. These terms all have well-defined meanings and it pays to spend five minutes learning what they are before rushing out to buy shares.

- *Inferred resources* are implied when the geologist does not have enough data to prove that the resource is continuous. In other words, the drilling or other sampling to date has shown patches of gold but they are too far apart and/or the sampling is insufficient to establish that they are all part of the same mineralised mass. There may be fracture zones or intrusive dikes in between. Obviously more exploration work needs to be done.
- *Indicated resources* again mean there is insufficient data to prove the resource is continuous, but this time the geologist reckons there's a reasonable expectation it is.
- *Measured resources* means they've now got enough data to prove it's continuous.

By the time we get to a reserve we are talking about a resource where under realistic conditions we can expect to mine the ground for a profit.

- *Probable reserves* are those where confidence is at a similar level to that for the indicated category of resources.
- *Proven reserves* mean that again they've got enough data to prove the orebody is continuous. At this point we've now definitely got a mine, unless the bottom drops out of the metal markets.

But remember, the difference between an inferred resource and a proven reserve can be several billion dollars.

Perhaps it should also be said that the orebody is never as regular as the drilling statements make it appear. Being three-dimensional it will have a strike length (the length over which it has been intercepted by drillholes), a width and a depth. As

112 THE NUMBERS GAME

Poseidon began to delineate Windarra in 1969, it had a minimum strike length of 330 metres, a width of 20 metres and was open at a depth of 130 metres. As the orebody is open at both ends and depth, let's say it's 500 metres long and 160 metres deep. Multiplying $500 \times 20 \times 160$ gives us a volume of 1.6 million cubic metres. If the ore averages 2.3 tonnes to the cubic metre that implies 3.68 million tonnes of ore. Take it down to 3.6 million. Average grades were 2.01 per cent nickel in the oxide zone and 2.52 per cent in the lower, sulphide zone. On the back of the envelope let's average those numbers at a grade of 2.25 per cent, which would mean the orebody contained 3.6 million $\times$ 0.0225 = 81 000 tonnes of nickel. Round it down to 75 000 tonnes.

That's a back of the envelope estimate of an orebody size. It's bound to be inaccurate because orebodies never come in neat cubic blocks. They pinch out, they form strata, they run along cracks and they are interrupted by big fracture zones and barren dikes. But the calculation is handy to give a speculator a ballpark idea of what the company might have.

Mining

In theory, once a measured reserve is established, it should be possible to bring a profitable mine into production. In practice, however, there is still no shortage of hazards. On the technical front, the ground may prove too unstable (incompetent, in mining argot) as happened at the initial shaft at BHP's Hartley platinum mine in Zimbabwe. Coal mines, particularly on the south coast of New South Wales, may prove to contain explosive pockets of methane gas. The US company Pegasus Gold Inc opened the Mt Todd goldmine in the Northern Territory but underestimated the hardness of the rock (the work index, to use more argot). That meant much of the ore had to be sent through the crushing circuit twice, blowing out the costs of treatment and making the mine uneconomical. Pegasus wrote off US$350 million.

Before the decision is taken to proceed with the mine, a company will normally make a feasibility study, taking all these factors into account. If the feasibility is only intended to satisfy the company management, it might be fairly brief. If it is intended to satisfy the company's bankers it will be considerably detailed.

One important calculation normally made around this stage will be of the mine's net present value (NPV). Let's say the prevailing interest rate is 5 per cent. If $100 million is invested at 5 per cent compound over five years it will grow to $128 million. To put that backwards, $100 million is the NPV of $128 million in five years' time. NPV is calculated by discounted cash flow (DCF) techniques. The net cash flows of the mine are calculated over, say, five years. If they come to $128 million and the prevailing interest rate is 5 per cent, the NPV of the mine is $100 million. If it is going to cost more than that to construct, it's uneconomical. Any big mine that hasn't been subjected to DCF techniques to calculate a NPV is a worry. There have been a few.

Finally there are, of course, human problems. An incompetent management can turn a viable mine into a loser. This is particularly likely where the mine is marginal—as many low-grade goldmines are—and there is little room for mistake. In the 1970s and 1980s many of Australia's biggest mines suffered greatly from wildcat union strikes and stoppages, particularly the iron ore mines of the Pilbara. There are also political hazards. The Jabiluka uranium mine in the Northern Territory was blocked from development for decades by legislation.

A good mine can produce great riches, but takes considerable skill to find and develop. A lucky exploration discovery may be an accident, but the successful development of a mine—especially a large one—is not. The companies who proceed to become large mining houses invariably demonstrate a high degree of expertise and judgment across a range of disciplines. The point can be illustrated by contrasting two stories from the nickel boom of the 1960s.

Early in 1966 Western Mining Corporation (WMC) struck three metres of massive sulphides containing 8.3 per cent nickel on the shores of Lake Lefroy in Western Australia. This was a sensational discovery but cannot be entirely attributed to luck. Westerns had historically been gold miners but had struggled to stay alive in the low price years of the 1960s. They sought to survive by looking at other minerals. Any prospector who found

114 THE NUMBERS GAME

an unusual rock around Kalgoorlie would be told by his mates to 'take it to Western Mining'. Westerns had also been running a systematic geological mapping program in the known mineralised area south of Kalgoorlie.

What was really lucky was the timing. Nickel prices were high at the time. Demand was high, mainly for stainless steel but also partly because of the Vietnam War, while supplies were sometimes restricted by union strikes at the leading producers in Canada. The rich discovery hole gave Westerns a window of opportunity if they were quick.

They were. If the men at the top of Westerns had been cautious they might have spent more time on exploration proving up reserves. But they realised that if the company was going to secure a place in the world nickel market—then dominated by only three suppliers—they had to move speedily. And the rich hole meant they should have enough ore down there to justify a shaft anyhow. In April the company announced it would develop a mine, which was brought into production rapidly under WMC's then deputy general manager in Western Australia, Arvi Parbo. 'We made some mistakes,' he recalled later. 'But mistakes can be corrected later and the important thing was to bring the mine in to catch the market'.[14]

One mistake was the new township of Kambalda. In its haste, WMC began building the town before anyone drilled the ground. When they did they discovered they were building the town over a rich orebody they called the Fisher Shoot. Kambalda suddenly became two townships as the rest of the houses were built a mile away on previously explored ground. Newcomers were often puzzled by the spectacle, in arid scrubland miles from anywhere, of a small town divided into two widely separated suburbs.

No modern Australian mine was ever brought into production more quickly than Kambalda. Shaft-sinking began on the Lunnon Shoot in July 1966. Construction of the concentrator began in October and by March 1967 the first ore was produced from the mines. The first consignment of concentrate was shipped overseas in August 1967. Westerns had won the race. By building a mine from scratch in nineteen months, they became a world power in the nickel market.

TYPES OF COMPANIES **115**

In contrast, consider what happened to Poseidon No Liability. Between 25 September and 30 September 1969, Poseidon shares jumped from $1.15 to $7. On the next day, 1 October, Poseidon released assays received to date from its discovery hole, PH–2, at Windarra. They showed a 40 foot intersection averaging 3.56 per cent nickel. The grade of 3.56 per cent nickel gave not only an impression of high grade but of high precision. The air of precision it gave was quite misleading, but it was allowed to stand for two months before any further grades were released. By that time Poseidon had run from $1 to $100 and had dragged the whole speculative market along in its wake.

It took several years and a Senate committee headed by Senator Peter Rae to discover the background to the first assay report. The assay laboratory, Geomin, had told Poseidon's consulting geologist, Geoff Burrill, that 30 out of 36 samples from the percussion hole had assayed greater than 1 per cent nickel. Later he phoned them again and was given some assay readings of between 2 and 5 per cent. All of them were rounded down and very approximate. That was all the evidence Burrill or Poseidon had when the board released a statement saying the intersection had averaged 3.56 per cent. This raised the question (never satisfactorily answered despite several hours of probing by the Senators) of how assays which were only approximated to round figures could have been recalculated to two decimal places. At one point the geologist, Geoff Burrill, said: 'Why on earth we came out with 3.56 I do not know. I wonder whether it was a misprint and should have been 3.50?'[15] Considering that the stock had gone from $1 to $100 on the basis of that assay, perhaps he should have shared his doubts with the market a bit earlier.

All that dreary evidence came years later. In 1969 Poseidon sparked probably the wildest share market boom in Australia's history. From $1 in September 1969, Poseidon shares soared to $280 by February 1970 and dragged a whole rag, tag and bobtail crowd of exploration stocks along in its wake.

The men at the top of Poseidon made several mistakes, but unlike WMC theirs weren't correctible. One of their biggest concerns was the threat of takeover so they built a defensive wall by placing shares into friendly hands. Those shares could have

THE NUMBERS GAME

been used to finance the development of the Windarra mine. Poseidon had hardly any cash when it struck Windarra. When its shares were soaring it should have raised cash by issuing equity, but the directors wanted to protect their ownership of Windarra, which meant the negotiations took too long and eventually the market went off the boil. The nickel price, which had been buoyed artificially in 1969 by union strikes in Canada, began falling. The fall was accelerated as new nickel mines came on stream around the world. Meanwhile Poseidon diverted precious capital into an ill-conceived project to reopen the old Burra copper mine in South Australia.

Windarra was not brought on stream until 1974, nearly five years after the original discovery. The contrast with WMC's urgency in 1966 is stark. By 1974 inflation had pushed up mining costs at a time when nickel prices had fallen. Windarra also had huge problems with incompetent rock surrounding the orebody. And the grade of 3.56 per cent turned out to be wrong. Poseidon's fabulous mine was a loser. In 1975, Poseidon went into receivership. The company was resuscitated later by Robert de Crespigny's Normandy group. When Windarra was finally developed—by WMC—the head grades averaged around 1.8 per cent, or roughly half the initial assay report which sent Poseidon to $280. And it was a dog of a mine, subject to vertical shearing and highly dangerous. Western Mining's chief executive, Hugh Morgan, told me years afterwards that if you didn't count the fact that it provided feed which Western Mining needed for its Kalgoorlie smelter, Windarra was only a break-even proposition. By itself it had never been worth mining.

Which makes it salutary to remember that at its height of $280 a share, Poseidon was capitalised at more than the Bank of New South Wales (now Westpac).

PREJUDICE 19

It takes luck to find a mine, but skill to develop one. Back mining companies with skilled management and stay away from ones whose management have proved they don't know what they're doing.

Financial analysis — exploration companies

The financial accounts of exploration and mining companies do not need a great deal of analysis as far as a lay investor is concerned. It is more important to understand the geology of the deposits and whether they are likely to be mined profitably.

With exploration company accounts, the only figures that matter are those detailing the amount of cash it has and the rate at which the cash is being spent. If a company has $1 million in the kitty and spending at the rate of $200 000 a quarter, then it's going to need more capital in fifteen months and will certainly start looking for it well before then. They don't wait until the last dollar is spent before they look for more. That company will either have to find something very soon or reduce its rate of exploration expenditure, which will not help its share price because it's less likely to find something if it's exploring less. Or it can dilute its equity in the prospect by going into a joint venture with a big brother. So cash backing is vital for an investor in an exploration company. The more cash it has, the longer it can survive and keep exploring. If it has little cash then it will probably soon be seeking more, which means that either:

- the investor will have to subscribe for more shares, increasing the commitment to the company; or
- the company will place shares with someone else, diluting the investor's equity; or
- the company will do a joint venture, again diluting the investor's equity.

Also try to calculate how much the company is spending to find its resources. In gold the rough rule of thumb is that successful companies have a finding cost of A$15 per ounce or less. So if a gold company spends $3 million on exploration, it should have found a resource containing at least 200 000 ounces.

Blue sky

Blue sky is hope. This term is most often used in mining, but it is applicable to all speculative companies. Let's say an exploration company is selling at 80 cents a share. Its cash backing is 20 cents per share and a realistic valuation of the various prospects it holds works out at another 15 cents—total, 35 cents. That means that at 80 cents, there is 45 cents worth of blue sky in the price. Blue sky is hope—hope that the prospect it is exploring will turn out to contain a bonanza, hope that the price of gold or nickel or whatever will jump, hope that the management are about to swing a great deal. Or maybe just sheer faith in astrology.

The difficult part of this calculation is working out what the mineral prospects are worth. If you can find a geologist who's been in the game for a while that's not hard. Just ask him how much he would pay for the prospects in question. As mining prospects are being traded all the time there's a more or less informed market and the geologist should be able to give a tolerably accurate estimate of their market value.

Exploration being an optimistic profession, all worthwhile exploration companies should have some blue sky in their price.

PREJUDICE 20

An exploration company that has no blue sky in its price is either a screaming bargain or has problems you don't know about yet. Better find out which before you buy the shares.

Financial analysis—mining companies

Mining company accounts can be opened right at the profit and loss statement. Did it make a profit last year and does it look like making one this year? Any worthwhile company will include in its accounts the unit cost of production of its minerals. If it is producing gold at US$250 an ounce, for example, and the spot price is holding above that, then the company should make a profit.

PREJUDICE 21

Once a company starts mining, it should swing into profit pretty quickly. If not, dive out.

A good mine should be profitable within a year of coming on stream, but the world abounds with mediocre mines—mines that didn't make their forecast profit last year for some reason but are going to get into the black next year and, meanwhile, would the shareholders mind subscribing to another rights issue?

The cash flow statement is worth checking to see whether the company is generating enough operating cash to meet its commitments in the current year. That cash flow can be augmented by the cash sitting in its current assets. Apart from that, an investor need not expend many brain cells trying to analyse the rest of the asset side of the balance sheet. The main assets will be its mines and prospects, which will be in at cost or valuation. These figures can be safely regarded as academic until the day a takeover raid happens.

Which raises the question: What value should be placed on a gold company in a takeover bid? The rule of thumb is A$25 per ounce of resource. So if an exploration company has a resource containing 200 000 ounces, a takeover price of $5 million is justifiable. If the company is actually mining the resource and has a mill established, the price goes up to A$50 per ounce. Those are the operative prices when the gold price was around A$450–500. They would tend to rise and fall with the A$ gold price.

Back to mining company accounts, the liabilities side of the balance sheet is more important than the assets. That is because debt has to be carefully structured. A mining company's expenditure on actual mining is relatively inflexible but the price it receives for minerals is volatile. A glance at the long-term price chart of any mine commodity will show it has fluctuated widely over the years and in the long term generally trends downward. Only a relative handful of mines can operate at low enough costs to be profitable through all mineral price cycles. Most mines are liable to become marginal or loss-makers during severe down cycles. A mining company which is financed purely by equity is in much better shape to endure down cycles than one which is financed by debt. If the worst comes to the worst, the mine can be put on care and maintenance until prices recover, during which time the company may be idle but will survive. But a company which is financed by debt may be ruined, because the

120 THE NUMBERS GAME

interest bill keeps ticking whether it is operating profitably or not, and once its cash is exhausted the lenders are liable to appoint a receiver.

Well-structured debt is a different proposition. In the 1960s, Conzinc Riotinto of Australia (CRA) borrowed money to finance the development of the Mt Tom Price iron ore mine. However, the loans were secured by contracts to export iron ore to Japan. This was brilliant innovative financing and quite secure. In principle, a similar concept was used to develop much of the Australian gold industry in the 1980s when financiers loaned money for mine development against the security of future production. Ensuring secure production entailed delineating adequate reserves and producing a feasibility plan for treatment. Again, this was secure lending. Gold loans were used aggressively by Australian miners and the mines they developed became a source of great prosperity and export income for the nation.

Hedging

The wife of British Labor leader Neil Kinnock refused to wear a gold wedding ring because she feared the gold might have come from apartheid South Africa. It is by no means clear how this refusal would have helped the blacks working in South Africa's gold mines, but Mrs Kinnock at least understood that gold is homogenous. A bar of refined gold from a South African mine is identical to one from Australia or Papua New Guinea. Gold's gold and that's that.

Together with its mystic, historical role as a unit of value, this homogeneity makes gold peculiarly suitable for hedging. The greatest risk in running any mine is that the metal being produced may fall in value. Gold mining companies can hedge against this risk by selling their gold forward. This assures them of a profit as long as the price at which they are selling is greater than their total cost of production.

In June 1999, Normandy's average cost of production was A$345 an ounce, which then equated to around US$225. (If depreciation and amortisation were counted in—a figure which Normandy published but very few other Australian miners were game to—the cost rose to A$442 or about US$300.) To the extent that Normandy could sell forward at prices greater than US$300, it was locking in future profits and ensuring its own survival, because by mid-1999 gold had gone below US$260 and looked to be out for the count. So Normandy sold forward and at June 1999 had a hedge book worth A$452 million, which was the surplus between the value of the hedge book if it had been closed out at 30 June and the prevailing low price of gold.

Note the important point that the hedge book will rise in value as the gold price falls, and vice versa. Let us say Normandy contracts to sell an ounce of gold forward for US$320. If the prevailing gold price is US$300 the value of that contract (ignoring transaction costs) is US$20. If the gold price falls to US$260, the value of the contract is US$60. Conversely, if the gold price rises to US$320 the value of the contract is zero and if it rises any further the value will go negative. But the fact that the value of the hedge book has fallen only represents an opportunity cost. Normandy is still making a US$20 guaranteed profit when the time comes to deliver the gold.

There's a lot of hype about hedge books but it helps if you remember that they're the insurance policy. When the gold price suddenly rebounded from US$260 to US$320 in September 1999, the value of the hedge books evaporated but the value of the gold companies' reserves in the ground increased. Normandy's Colin Jackson said: 'If I had to choose between having gold at US$260 and a hedge book worth $452 million or gold at US$320 and a hedge book worth zero, that's a pretty easy choice'.[16] Very easy, because Normandy's hedge book only represented about 15 per cent of its reserves.

Australian gold companies now give considerable detail on their hedge books, and they are worth studying because the hedge book structure has become an important feature. A company which does not hedge at all is taking a risk on the future gold price. If it soars the company will enjoy a bonanza, but if it falls the company may have to close its mines.

When looking at the structure of a hedge book, it is valuable to distinguish between obligations and rights. A forward sale is an obligation to deliver gold at a specified price at a specified date. A put option, however, is a right to sell gold at a future date. If the prevailing price is higher at that date than the price specified in the put option, the company can simply let the option expire and sell the gold spot. So when looking at the value of a hedge book, it is worth remembering that the obligations will have to be met but the rights can be waived if the price rises.

The Newcrest hedge book in 1999 contained a large proportion of granted call options. These are best regarded as obligations because the right to exercise lay with the parties to whom Newcrest had granted the calls. Newcrest collected premiums by granting these calls, which offset the premiums it had to pay to buy put options. Transactions such as these made the Newcrest hedge book quite complicated. Anyone who could understand it would have had an intellect worthy of nuclear physics or brain surgery.

When looking at a hedge book, the lay reader can be forgiven for wondering who buys gold forward at such huge prices. Sons of Gwalia, for example, had forward sales in 1999 rising well over A$600 per ounce at a time when the prevailing gold price was only half that level. No, these are not jewellers safeguarding future inventory. The gold hedging market has absolutely nothing to do with physical supply and demand. It is entirely based on interest rate differentials.

The usual mechanics of a forward sale begin with a central bank. Central banks have gold laying around their vaults as a sterile asset, earning nothing. In the 1980s some miners and bullion brokers saw the opportunity to gain from this. In a typical transaction, a broker such as Rothschild with a mining company client would go to a central bank and offer to borrow gold from it at a leasing rate of 1 per cent. The bank jumped at the chance to get 1 per cent on an asset which was otherwise earning nothing and just occupying space.

The broker immediately sold the gold (there are actually no forward sales, only spot sales) and reinvested the money in a riskless security such as a US T-bond at maybe 8 per cent for whatever the term of the forward was supposed to be. The broker might take 2 per cent commission, the bank got its 1 per cent leasing rate and the remaining 5 per cent was compounded as the return to the miner. Over five or ten years that compounded into a handsome price.

For nearly two decades everyone was happy. The central bank got 1 per cent on an otherwise sterile asset, the broker made commission and the gold miner had locked in a future profit. It was such a good game that speculators got into the act, notably the notorious New York hedge funds. A speculator selling gold short follows exactly the same process as a gold miner. The important differential is that the speculator doesn't have any gold in the ground. As long as the gold price falls—or even stays much the same—the speculator makes money. If the gold price rises, however, the speculator cannot deliver and must settle in cash and will be liable to margin calls. The speculator will also suffer if leasing rates rise or T-bond rates fall. When this happened in September 1999—and central banks simultaneously decided to freeze the amount of gold they were lending—the short sellers were caught in a short but nasty squeeze. Finally, when a company which can produce a metal at a cost of $USX sells it forward at $USX + $US50, it has only hedged half its risk. It has covered itself against risk on the metal price, but not on any future variations in the $US against the $A. Most resource companies which hedge their metal therefore also hedge the currency. Unfortunately, this cannot be done with the same degree of certainty because currencies can fluctuate widely and not always for logical reasons. Currency hedges have to be managed very carefully or they can be disastrous, as many resource companies found to their peril between the late 1990s and early 2000s. Australia's biggest zinc miner, Pasminco, went into administration because of bad currency hedging.

Oil and gas companies

Broadly oil and gas companies operate on the same principles as mining companies except that they deal in fluids instead of solids and their assets are oil and gas reservoirs instead of orebodies. These reservoirs typically occur in sedimentary basins well below the earth's surface—and frequently below the seabed.

In putting together the following information on oil and gas exploration and development I have used some material from Dr Victor Rudenno's authoritative *Mining Valuation Handbook—for Projects, Companies and Shares* (Wrightbooks, 1998). Any

124 THE NUMBERS GAME

reader who wants to study further the economics of mining and oil should buy a copy of this excellent book.[17]

Listed oil companies are required to make announcements to the Australian Stock Exchange providing information on the success or failure of their exploration wells. Dry holes are plugged and abandoned. In more promising holes, the company may provide some data on the thickness of the reservoir and the net pay (the proportion of the reservoir containing permeable sands that may flow oil and gas).

Typically the oil will be above the water in the sandstone formation. A key question when analysing the well is whether the pressure from the water will be sufficient to drive the oil and gas to the surface when the reservoir is tapped.

The company may run repeat formation tests to collect samples of the fluids. If these are promising, the company may run one or more drill stem tests. These isolate the discovery zone (or zones) in the well and allow oil and gas to flow through tubing to the surface.

Drill stem test announcements should be read carefully. The two key factors are the time taken and the size of the choke—the valve at the top of the well through which the fluids flow. From the rate at which oil and gas flows in a drill stem test, the company may extrapolate the number of barrels of oil or cubic metres of gas the well would flow per day. But before taking this extrapolation at face value it is worth checking how the well was tested.

If a well maintains a strong flow rate for several hours through a large choke, we may well be looking at a commercial field. However, a mendacious company might make a small, weak discovery look strong by running it for only a short time through a small choke. Pressure is important. If the basin does not have enough driving pressure to push the hydrocarbons out of their own accord, then more expensive means will have to be used such as water injection which may well make the field uneconomical. If water is recovered in a test, it could be because the test was run near the point where the oil and water meet.

Rudenno points out that the presence of drilling mud in a test can be a warning signal. He says:

While drilling the well, mud will be pumped down the well to ensure that reservoir pressure will not force the drill stem out of the well and result in oil or gas blowing out onto the surface as is often shown in the movies [the celebrated, but anachronistic, gusher]. If the pressure from the mud is too great, it may be forced into the reservoir and cause damage. Therefore any mud acquired during testing may suggest over-pressure during drilling and potentially damaged formation.[18]

Oil and gas reserves

Unlike minerals, the term 'resources' is not applied when measuring oil and gas deposits. They are stated as reserves and come in five categories. The highest are simply called 'reserves'. These are volumes of hydrocarbons that should be economically recoverable. After that, in order of certainty, they are ranked as follows:

- *Proved reserves*—estimated with reasonable certainty to be economically recoverable.
- *Unproved reserves*—based on similar data to those that are proven, except that there are some technical, regulatory or economic uncertainties.
- *Probable reserves*—less certain than proved reserves, but can be estimated with enough certainty to indicate they are more likely to be recovered than not.
- *Possible reserves*—less certain. It cannot be said whether they are more likely to be recovered than not.

The following glossary may help readers to better understand oil and gas reserve calculations:

- *Area of closure*—the area of the structure that is expected to contain oil. Petroleum geologists will estimate this area before drilling. After drilling, their preliminary estimates are sometimes found to have been wrong by a considerable factor.
- *Net pay*—the vertical height of the potential oil column. Initially this is estimated from the seismic and geological data derived from other wells in the particular basin.

126 THE NUMBERS GAME

- *Porosity*—the voids or spaces in the sandstone particles which contain the oil. The porosity is usually cited as a fraction of the sandstone. Typical porosity ranges between 1 and 40 per cent with the most common levels around 20 to 30 per cent.
- *Permeability*—the ability of the hydrocarbons (and any accompanying water) to flow through the voids.
- *Recovery factor*—this is a factor of the rock's permeability measured in millidarcies (range of 1 to 1000 with typical levels in excess of 100) and the pressure and driving forces such as water that will dictate the amount recovered. For oilfields typical recovery factors are between 10 and 40 per cent, although they can be as high as 70 per cent. For gas the range is typically 50 to 80 per cent.
- *Hydrocarbon saturation*—the proportion of oil associated with water in the structure. Typical levels are 50 per cent to 90 per cent.
- *Shrinkage factor*—oil shrinks due to the loss of higher fractions as the pressure drops when it rises from the reservoir to the stock tank.
- *Expansion factor*—by contrast, gas expands 50 to 350 times as it reaches the surface.

Multiplying all these factors gives the volume of oil and gas which can be recovered from a structure. It is rare, however, for an oil company to give enough data in its announcements for an investor to be able to do the calculation. Rudenno gives the following example:

Area of closure = 8.5 square kilometres
Net pay = 15 metres
Porosity = 30 per cent
Recovery factor = 35 per cent
Hydrocarbon saturation = 85 per cent
Shrinkage factor = 95 per cent
Barrels of oil per cubic metre = 6.38
Therefore recoverable oil in place = 6.38 × 8.5 × 10(6) × 0.15 × 0.3 × 0.85 × 0.95 = 69 million barrels

Oil and gas recovery

Whereas minerals have to be forcibly extracted from the earth, oil and gas simply flow out. Sometimes they flow under natural pressure, but sometimes they need assistance. Water may be injected into the reservoir to help drive hydrocarbons out. Small explosive charges may be inserted in the reservoir (called fraccing) to improve permeability.

Production from an oil field will decline over time as the pressure weakens. Until the company knows the rate of decline, the usual assumption is that it will decline at a rate of 15 to 20 per cent a year. However, secondary measures to stimulate flow can keep fields operating for very long times. The classic case is Barrow Island, off Australia's west coast, which has been producing oil since 1967.

An offshore oil and gas production platform is the size of a very large skyscraper and commensurately expensive. By contrast an onshore field may be brought on stream relatively cheaply, especially if it is close to an existing pipeline. And once the oil and gas start flowing through the pipeline, the cash starts streaming in. A small gasfield can be quite a nice business. Maintenance is low and it just keeps ticking away producing money day and night.

Biotechs

If the market goes white hot about biotech stocks, as it did in 1999–2000, the smartest thing an ordinary investor can do is sell and run, because otherwise it's likely to be a very long haul.

A dotcom with a bright idea or application can be started in a garage (like Cisco) and—with genius and hard work—generate riches very quickly. But however many geniuses are running a biotech company, the riches are a long way distant. Biotechs can be divided into two types: those that are trying to break into the pharmaceutical market and those with products aimed at the less-regulated over-the-counter market. The best way to understand the hurdles is to look at the pharmaceutical market first.

The time lag between some scientist having an idea and the actual commercial cash flow from it can be a decade or more.

Typically, Ungobungo tribe has always known that the Ungo-bungo plant has healing properties. In the backroom of some university, Professor Algae sweats away trying to isolate the particular molecule that gives the plant those properties, so that he can then take it to market and make a million dollars. One of the most difficult cases on record was the commercialisation of Taxol, the first drug used to treat ovarian cancer. It is extracted from the bark of the American yew tree, but it took scientists 10 years to discover how to synthesise it.

The word 'synthesise' raises another problem. Most drugs are derived from chemicals that occur in nature. Your garden probably contains several plants with properties that are medicinal or lethal (the common oleander being an example of the latter). Typically a scientist will begin by isolating the molecule that gives a plant or animal its peculiar properties. If the plant or animal is commonplace it might be possible to harvest or breed it naturally. But if the drug is to be manufactured on any scale and be reliably replicated, the molecule will have to be synthesised and that adds another dimension to the problem. One large hurdle is proving that the drug can be manufactured consistently and reliably, so that this month's batch is the same as last month's batch.

Having isolated the molecule, synthesised it and manufactured it, the next hurdle will be the pre-clinical trial. These are conducted on animals, usually mice, to see whether the drug is safe and what its side effects are. For a new drug, pre-clinical trials might typically take at least two years.

Assuming the pre-clinical trials go well and the drug is established as safe, the next step will be clinical trials where the drug is tested on humans. These are in three phases. The first phase uses volunteers and is aimed at making sure the drug really is safe for humans. Phase one might take about a year. Phase two comprises treatment of 100 to 200 people suffering from the disease the drug is designed to attack. A control group might or might not be used depending on the circumstances. If it's an anti-cancer drug, for example, a control group would not be used because that would be tantamount to letting them die for the sake of making a comparison. Phase two might take two years.

TYPES OF COMPANIES **129**

Phase three consists of larger trials (anything from 200 to 2000 patients) conducted in public hospitals. Before the hospital will allow a company to make the trials, the results of phase two have to be evaluated and written up, a process that could easily take six months. The point of phase three is that the drug is now being used under real world conditions, whereas phases one and two are conducted in more controlled conditions.[19]

Looking at this whole process it is easy to see how a company could spend a decade before getting approval to take its drug to market. The rules are predominantly set by the US Federal Drug Administration. The FDA prides itself on protecting consumers. However, if the FDA did not exist, the major drug companies would have invented it. The approval process is so time consuming and takes such deep pockets, that no small company could survive it without having to call for help. So the big pharmaceutical companies are perched over the approval process, waiting for a small company to come up with a good idea. When it falters for lack of money, the big birds spread their vulture wings and pounce. Some small biotechs survive the ordeal to become big ones, but the trail is littered with the bones of those who didn't.

There are some exceptions. If a drug is an extension of one that is already proven safe, the time taken for approval can be shortened dramatically. The FDA is also prepared to fast-track a drug that has 'orphan' status. Orphan drugs are those designed to treat conditions where the market is too small for the majors. The definition of an orphan drug is one for a condition where there are only likely to be 200 000 patients or fewer a year. That allows some room for small companies. Ovarian cancer falls within that definition, for instance.

By FDA standards approval can be rapid for orphan drugs. Glovec, which treats one of the less common forms of leukaemia, did a phase two study in 35 patients, achieved remission in 33 of them, and was approved by the FDA in two and a half years. Biotechs need patient capital because overheads are high. Novogen spent three years getting its anti-cancer drug Phenoxidol through phase two trials and by that time had spent maybe $6 million. If it had to conduct the trials in the USA, rather than Australia, they would have cost a multiple of that sum.

130 THE NUMBERS GAME

Biotechs are a field where an investor really needs expert assistance. If the biotech company is working on an orphan drug it's chances are much better than if it is a mainstream one, but the investor needs to know the difference. There are other hazards too. Is the new drug really a breakthrough, or does it only stop a cold one day earlier than existing treatments? If it's only a 5 per cent improvement on what's on the shelves already, nobody's going to get too excited.

If a broker is giving you a hard sell about an exciting new drug invented by some biotech, ask him for its therapeutic index. This is the ratio of the dose that causes harm to the dose that gets a beneficial effect. In something like aspirin the index is probably something like 15:1 or 20:1. That is, a patient would have to take 15 or 20 times the recommended dosage before he or she was harmed by it. In an anti-cancer drug, however, the ratio might be 1.5:1. The lower the index, the riskier the drug.

The rewards in pharmaceuticals can be magnificent, and Australians are quite skilled in this field, but the hurdles are high. That's why some biotechs don't even attempt the hurdles, but decide to make complementary medicines instead, such as vitamins.

One glance around your local health shop will tell you that this is an overcrowded market. Prices of vitamins are high in the health shops, but not much of that goes to the makers. The retail prices really reflect the retail, wholesale and manufacturers' margins. Blackmores, which has been in the game for 60 years, was making NPAT of about $5 million in 2002 on $80 million sales. That's a nice margin, but nothing terrific. Companies such as that can be valued as normal industrials.

Worse, in the wake of the Pan Pharmaceuticals disaster of 2003, there was every likelihood that regulators were going to get a lot tougher on the over-the-counter market.

The range of company types that has been overviewed in this chapter is not exhaustive, but covers most of the types that were popular at the time of writing.

Fashions change in companies. In 1990 there was hardly a tech stock on the Australian boards. By 2000 they had grown like weeds. To take another example, a book on security analysis written in 1900 in the US or the UK would have devoted much of its space to railroad stocks. If this book goes to further editions, and some new genus of company becomes fashionable enough to examine, that will be included too.

4

Managed investments

Managed investments is a new term for an old type of investment. They have also been restructured under the *Managed Investments Act 1999*, and it is important that investors understand how their protection has been weakened.

Units in a fund or trust are a form of equity. The owners of the units share in all the profits. Unlike a company, however, the owners of the units have almost no say in the management.

Until recently, a fund or trust was run by the manager. The manager's powers were limited by the trust deed, which would typically lay down limits on borrowing and the types of investment the manager could make. A trustee was appointed with the responsibility of enforcing that trust deed. Typically the trustee controlled the cheque book. Before the management company could buy a property or a block of shares it had to get the trustee's approval. If the trust collapsed, the manager could be sued by the trustee on behalf of the unitholders. The unitholders also had the right to sue the trustee for falling asleep at the wheel—if trust deed covenants had been breached and the trustee had tolerated the breach or hadn't noticed it.

Over the decades this system worked tolerably well. There weren't too many notable disasters until the Estate Mortgage group of trusts collapsed in 1990. The trustee of Estate Mortgage was Burns Philp Trustee, a subsidiary of one of Australia's oldest and—until then—most respected companies. Irate unitholders sued not only Burns Philp Trustee but its parent company Burns Philp & Co.

132

In the wake of that collapse, the government decided to kill off trustees and alter the entire nature of unit trusts. Trustees were accused of being lazy and ineffective. Maybe some had been, but overall the system hadn't worked too badly and the cost of trustees was fairly small.

Under the *Managed Investments Act*, the role of trustees was abolished. Trusts and funds were renamed 'managed investments'. The trust deed was abolished to be replaced by a 'constitution'. The manager, or management company, was renamed the 'single responsible entity'. The single responsible entity, or SRE, now has complete power. An SRE can invest however it likes, providing it is in accordance with the constitution (most of which, in practice, are the old trust deeds with a few necessary changes). The legislation provides that compliance with the constitution is ensured by having either a compliance committee or a majority of independent directors on the board of the management company.

PREJUDICE 22

Independent directors have historically proved almost useless whenever faced by a strong-minded management.

These safeguards were less than totally reassuring. Time and again when companies hit trouble (Westpac in the 1980s and BHP in the 1990s) the so-called independent directors on the board seem to have been largely helpless in controlling management or protecting investors. The classic case is the State Bank of South Australia (SBSA), where an entire board of independent directors was overrun by the bank's chief executive, Tim Marcus Clark, for several years. The SBSA's collapse in 1991 resulted in the largest loss in Australia's corporate history.

Proponents of the *Managed Investments Act* say that it has removed the confusion about the respective roles of managers and trustees. It also places clear liability upon the manager in the event of fraud.

Well, the trustee–manager relationship had been around for a century and to any participant in the markets it did not seem to be causing much confusion. On the liability question, it may be instructive to ponder for a second what would have happened had the *Managed Investments Act* been in force when Estate Mortgage collapsed. The SRE would have been the management company, which was comprehensively broke. Its principals, Richard and Reuben Lew, were bankrupt and in prison. Unitholders would have had a clear lawsuit but it would have been futile because they would have collected absolutely zilch. Instead, they were able to sue the trustee company and its parent and eventually collected some $100 million.

A trustee had the pre-emptive power to stop a manager doing something wrong. Under the new legislation, unitholders will be able to take action only after the manager has done something wrong. There is a great difference between preventing an act from happening and trying to retrieve money after the act has happened.

Even if unitholders believe that a manager has run off the rails, they will only be able to remove the manager in extreme circumstances. It is much easier to remove a director (or even a board) of a company than a manager of a trust.

In these changed circumstances, it pays investors in funds and trusts to be wary. The best insurance is to invest only where the single responsible entity has a long and proven record of probity, as well as performance.

PREJUDICE 23

A single responsible entity should be treated as guilty until proven innocent. An honest track record of managing investments for a decade is the minimum to make one acceptable.

Funds

Funds are still the largest area of investment in Australia. At the end of 1999 there was $561 billion under management in Australian funds—up from $470 billion a year earlier. There is a huge array of choice. Their names usually give a good indication of their main investments.

MANAGED INVESTMENTS **135**

- *Cash management trusts*—typically these invest in bonds and bank bills. They should be quite safe, although the yields can be unexciting in times of low interest rates.
- *Fixed interest funds*—invest in a wider range of fixed interest securities. Some specifically invest in bonds.
- *Equity funds*—invest purely in equities. Some purely in Australian equities.
- *International equity funds*—invest in international equities. Some are country or region specific, such as Asia funds, European funds, US funds or Japanese funds.
- *Balanced funds*—a mix of international and Australian equities and fixed interest.

Funds can be further divided into those that aim for growth and those that aim for income. There are also analysts who rank and rate the various funds, which saves the investor a great deal of time and research. The first choice an investor should make is to decide what type of fund best suits his or her needs. A financial advisor can then provide a list of the best-performing funds of that type. There are also several websites that provide the same service.

Let's say an investor wanted a fund specialising in Australian equities with at least three years' track record. The *Australian Financial Review* trading room page of 19 May 2003 listed the top Australian share funds ranked by size (see Table 4.1).

Note that these fund performances—and hence rankings— will change month by month. Funds which are denominated as wholesale are normally for institutions and require a minimum investment of $100 000 or more. The entry prices into funds are normally a few percentage points above the exit prices.

The performance table shows a large variation between the funds. The three years to May 2003 were a tough time in the Australian share market as it came off the highs of the dotcom boom. This is a good testing time for fund managers. Almost any fool can make money in a rising market, but it takes good management to produce a better return in a tough one. But as usual in investment, nothing is simple. The individuals and teams who achieve these performances tend to move about between funds. Tracking the movements of the best fund managers is a

136 THE NUMBERS GAME

Table 4.1 Largest Australian share funds as at 19 May 2003

	Name	Size ($m)	3 year performance (%)	5 year performance (%)
1	Colonial First State Wholesale Imputation Fund	4 560	3.98	8.55
2	Colonial First State Imputation Fund	2 877	2.79	7.37
3	Perpetual Wholesale Industrial Share Fund	2 453	8.82	9.16
4	Maple-Brown Abbott Australian Equity Fund	2 408	11.17	8.59
5	Perpetual's Industrial Share Fund	2 369	7.84	8.15
6	UBS Global Asset Management Australian Share Fund	1 389	6.6	9.03
7	Merrill Lynch Wholesale Imputation Fund	1 323	0.66	4.42
8	Colonial First State Wholesale Australian Share Fund	1 304	1.41	5.93
9	Vanguard Australian Shares Index Fund	832	2.6	4.8
10	Schroder Australian Equities	721	3.01	7.47

minor industry and you need to be sure that the chaps who achieved the best figures over the past three years are still in place. Also, while Maple-Brown Abbott has consistently been one of Australia's top fund managers for many years, you need a minimum of $500 000 to invest.

Adverse markets are the best test of good fund managers, because Blind Freddie can making money in rising markets.

Management expense ratio (MER) is calculated by taking the total amount of fees deducted from the fund plus all expenses recovered from or paid out of the fund, and expressing it as a percentage of the average fund size for the period under review. MERs are required by law to be included in managed fund prospectuses. Typically a management company will charge an entry fee to investors. Thus if an investor puts $10 000 into a fund where the entry fee is 3 per cent, the investor loses $300 straight off the top and his or her investment is really only $9700. The manager will also take a management fee of maybe 1.5 per cent a year as well. Sometimes the investor is offered a choice of no entry fee but a higher management fee. The management fee can be easily borne in funds which are earning 15 per cent or more. But when a manager is under-performing, the fees really bite. See Table 4.2 for a guide to average MERs.

PREJUDICE 24

Any manager charging 2 per cent for expertise had better be pretty expert. The alternative is to invest directly in the sector. If you can do 98 per cent as well as the manager, you're square with the game.

Property trusts

One of the most popular forms of managed investment in Australia over the decades has been the property trust. Many people would regard them as an investment in property, but mostly they're not. True, if a trust sells assets during a property boom it will show a profit just like a property company. But outside of boomtime, property trusts are more accurately regarded as fixed interest investments.

A property trust typically has a portfolio of commercial, industrial or retail properties. Some concentrate in one sector, some have a mixture.

Property trust accounts are pretty straightforward to read, or should be anyway. The three key factors to the performance of

138 THE NUMBERS GAME

Table 4.2 Average management expense ratios, 2003

Investment	Rate (%)
Australian equity trusts—diversified	1.81
Australian equity trusts—property	1.53
Australian equity trusts—small companies	2.15
Australian equity trusts—resources	2.04
Cash trusts	0.98
Fixed interest trusts—diversified	1.31
International equity trusts—Asia inc. Japan	2.45
International equity trusts—Asia ex Japan	2.23
International equity trusts—diversified	1.90
International equity trusts—Japan	2.09
International equity trusts—North America	2.19
International equity trusts—Western Europe	2.01
International fixed interest trusts—diversified	1.90
Mortgage trusts—diversified	1.26
Multi-sector trusts—Aggressive	1.89
Multi-sector trusts—balanced	1.89
Multi-sector trusts—defensive	1.65
Multi-sector trusts—growth	1.89
Multi-sector trusts—moderate	1.70
United property trusts—diversified	1.56

Source: Morningstar Research, Investment & Financial Services
Association, 2003

any property trust will be its level of gearing, its vacancy rate
and the terms of its leases.

PREJUDICE 25

Avoid geared, unlisted property trusts.

Gearing makes a property trust more vulnerable. A rise in
interest rates will erode its profits. So will a fall in its rental
income. Such investment vehicles are particularly prone to
trouble in credit squeezes. When interest rates rise suddenly, the
trust's costs will rise proportionately. Then as the credit squeeze

bites into the commercial sector, tenants will quit their premises, slashing the trust's income. The trust may very well collapse—many have in past credit squeezes.

It's bad enough when this happens in a listed trust, but at least investors have some chance to bale out on the way down. Units in unlisted trusts are usually illiquid, which means that in a crisis the investors are trapped.

By way of contrast let's look at the accounts of General Property Trust (GPT), which has earned a reputation as a leader in the property trust industry. The 1999 annual report showed total assets of $4.8 billion against total liabilities of $924 million. Gearing was therefore 19.3 per cent. Of that $924 million, $770 million was debt and the rest provisions and accounts payable.

Total revenue (excluding sales of properties) was $450 million. Expenses were $175 million, giving a profit of $275 million. The revenue therefore represented a yield of 9.4 per cent on the $4.8 billion assets, which is satisfactory for a group of GPT's size. Profit margin was 5.7 per cent. Basic earnings per unit were 18.8 cents. Net asset backing per unit was $2.51.

As mentioned earlier, one of the key factors in a property trust is the vacancy rate. In practice, it is difficult to achieve 100 per cent occupancy of a suite of properties, because there is always some shop or office that has just been vacated. GPT came close at the end of the 1999 calendar year, however. Its annual report is a model for property trusts, listing all relevant statistics for each of the properties under its management. Most were well over 90 per cent and a few were 100 per cent. The lowest occupancy rate was 87 per cent for Allendale Square in Perth.

Naturally, the vacancy rate is of little comfort if all the leases are going to expire soon after balance date. GPT's annual report also showed the proportion of leases expiring in each of the forthcoming years. In most cases, the leases did not expire for five years or more, and were often held by leading Australian and international companies.

The downside to a high occupancy rate is that there is little room for a trust's income to grow. But the income stream is strong and that helps an investor to sleep soundly at nights. It usually pays to go for quality and safety in a property trust even if the return is a little lower than those being offered by some of the fancier ones. Don't expect much growth in the unit price. Buy property trusts for the income stream and do your gambling in other bits of the portfolio.

5

Prospectuses

PREJUDICE 26

A rising market makes any prospectus a good prospectus.

When the market is running hot, as it was in 1999, applying traditional financial analysis to a prospectus is a waste of precious brain cells. When the market is enthusiastic and undiscriminating, stocks are liable to list at a premium—or go for a run after listing—regardless of their intrinsic value or future earnings.

As one example out of many from 1999, take HotCopper. The core business of this company was Australia's most popular financial chat page on the Internet. In the period between January and August 1999, when it floated, HotCopper's income generated from its Net pages was just $5450—and no, there are no noughts missing from that figure.

On the strength of the fact that it was going to generate advertising from its pages and was going to launch into Internet-related businesses, HotCopper raised $5 million from the public. The shares were issued at 30 cents and opened at 35 cents when it listed. In early 2000 they ran as high as 64 cents.

Good luck to HotCopper and the punters aboard her, but its prospectus really didn't contain much except hope and $5450. Yet at its peak price in early trading the company was capitalised at $27 million, and punters who took shares in the prospectus had doubled their money.

141

142 THE NUMBERS GAME

PREJUDICE 27

The definition of a prospectus in a boom is 'the fat bit in front of the application form'.

In a hot market, the trick is not to analyse a prospectus but to get hold of one with a live application form. Conversely, when the market is in a sour mood, even quite desirable companies may struggle to get floated. So before deciding to take up shares in a prospectus, the first judgment to be made is about the state of the market. Even if the float looks pretty hopeless, in a hot market it may be worth taking up shares on the ground that if you take bad floats from your broker, he may let you in on a good one later.

Also, the market has to be hot for the particular type of stock. In 1999 technology stocks were running wild, so just about any prospectus that mentioned the Internet or telecommunications was successful. On the other hand, traditional industrial stocks enjoyed only ordinary acceptance and speculative mining stocks were at a heavy discount. The prospectus for Tin Australia NL struggled to meet its minimum subscription and the shares which had been issued at 26 cents traded as low as 2.5 cents after listing. But then it discovered a technology for cleaning acid mine drainage, changed its name to Virotec and the shares shot to $1.60.

Analysis

If the market is not in one of its hot phases, it becomes advisable to actually read the prospectus. Prospectuses can be analysed in the same way as ordinary company accounts, except that there are a few extra points to watch. What is the first point to check?

Who are the directors?

If they are people of probity who have a track record of success in business, it is often safe to subscribe without checking much further. If any of them have been touched by scandal, it is probably unsafe. If you don't know them, ask around. If someone says of a director: 'he used to be a bit fleet of foot, but he's gone straight now', throw the prospectus into the universal filing unit.

PREJUDICE 28

In business, leopards *never* change their spots.

Is it a prospectus?

If the document which has arrived in the mail is a prospectus it should say so somewhere in the first few pages, in a statement which should also give its date of issue. Or it may be an information memorandum. Broadly, a *prospectus* is issued to raise money for the purposes of a company, while an *information memorandum* is issued by existing shareholders in a company who want to sell their shares to the public—an important distinction to which we shall return. If the document doesn't claim to be either a prospectus or an information memorandum and is seeking your money, it pays to be very wary. The prospectus laws of Australia are pretty tough but investors can lose the protection of them if they subscribe to a document that is not a prospectus.

Will the investment expose subscribers to any further liability?

In a limited liability company, shareholders are not liable to pay any more than the outstanding unpaid liability (if any) on their shares. If the shares they buy are fully paid, there can be no further liability. If the company then goes broke, the shareholders owe the creditors nothing.

Sometimes shares are issued partly paid. These are known as *contributing shares*. Aztec Exploration caused a great deal of grief to shareholders when it floated in 1981 with its 50 cent shares paid to 20 cents. Nine months later it called 15 cents of the unpaid 30 cents. The shares dropped to 2 cents as holders quit rather than pay the call. To cite another example, the second tranche of Telstra was finely priced. The instalment receipts, as they were called, were issued at $4.50 with a further $2.90 to pay a year later. The terms meant that the receipts became a losing

144 THE NUMBERS GAME

proposition whenever the fully paid Telstra shares dipped below $7.40, which they later did.

No liability shares mean exactly what they say. Subscribers have no liability to pay future calls and instead can forfeit their holdings. Forfeited shares become the property of the company, which sells them for whatever it can raise. (Forfeited share sales can be an interesting way of acquiring a cheap entry into a speculative company.)

Unlimited liability stock is rarely seen today, for excellent reasons. When an unlimited liability company fails, the creditors have unlimited recourse against the assets of the shareholders, who can lose everything. This happened when Dr Michael Garretty's Dividend Fund Inc collapsed in 1971. Shareholders, many of whom had been sold their stock by door-to-door salespeople, were horrified to learn they could lose their cars and houses to creditors, who included Dr Garretty.

How much are the vendors taking?

We should be realistic about vendors. Normally a prospectus is drawn up to float a business or collection of mining leases or some other asset being sold into the company by the vendors. No vendor ever spent a lifetime building up a business so that he or she could then sell it to the public for less than it was worth. So subscribers should expect to pay some sort of premium in return for being allowed to own part of the enterprise. The individuals or seed capitalists who put the early work and money into the enterprise deserve some reward for developing it to the point where it is worth floating. However, it is up to the subscribers to decide whether it is worth floating at all. That decision will depend on several factors, of which the vendor consideration will be an important one.

Somewhere in the prospectus should be a table showing what the issued capital of the company will look like assuming all the money is raised. This should show how much of the company the public shareholders will have after listing compared to how much the vendors and other parties will hold. Once upon a time, vendors either took cash or shares for injecting their business or mineral prospect into a prospectus. By 1999 they were getting greedy. Not only were they taking cash for the business but they were retaining a heavy chunk of shares in the public company as well. Of the 112 companies floated in 1999, vendors retained 50 per cent or more of the equity in 79.[1] In technology stocks, the average was around 70 per cent retained by vendors. In many cases, the public were putting up all the money but the vendors were retaining control.

Is money going to the company or the vendors?

In a float, the money subscribed for shares becomes part of the assets of the company. In a share sale, the money is paid to the vendors in return for their shares. Sometimes the two elements are mixed, with some of the money going to the company and some to take out shares held by the vendors. It is important to distinguish between these two. Money subscribed to the company stays in the company and (hopefully) will be used to the advantage of the company of which you are now a part-owner. Money used to buy out vendors is gone forever.

Is the business fairly priced?

The prospectus should contain abbreviated accounts showing what the business looked like before it was floated and pro forma accounts showing what it will look like after the money has been raised. The normal purpose of a raising is to extinguish all or a lot of the debt, so the pro forma balance sheet should show more cash and less debt.

Also look at the net assets of the company as it was before the float. That represents the approximate value of the business which the promoters are selling. How does that compare with what they are taking in vendor consideration and with what subscribers are being asked to pay?

Before signing a cheque for the shares, it is worth a subscriber doing five minutes arithmetic by comparing the stake the public shareholders will have with the value of the asset that the vendors are injecting into the company. Almost any prospectus for a tech stock in 1999 would serve as an example, but let's take

146 THE NUMBERS GAME

ChaosMusic. The prospectus showed that if the shares were floated at $1.50, the ownership would be as shown in Table 5.1.

Table 5.1 ChaosMusic prospectus (indicated capital structure)

	No. of shares	% of company
Existing shareholders	15.25m	56.1
New shareholders	10.0m	36.8
Others	1.9m	7.1
Totals	27.2m	100.0

That was assuming a $1.50 share price was achieved. ChaosMusic was floated by a *bookbuild*. This is a form of auction in which the subscribers bid to determine the final price of the shares. The ultimate price achieved was $1.40, which meant the new shareholders (the public) held about 10.7 million shares representing 38 per cent of the company. However, let's work on Table 5.1 because that was all the information the public had to work with when making their decision to subscribe.

The float was aimed at raising $15 million from the public, so that was the amount the 10 million shares would represent. It also meant the public got only 36.9 per cent of ChaosMusic. The existing shareholders would still retain majority control with 56.1 per cent. So the existing shareholders' equity was capitalised at nearly $23 million.

The pro forma balance sheet in the prospectus showed what ChaosMusic would look like after the float. It's reproduced in Table 5.2.

Table 5.2 ChaosMusic pro forma balance sheet (projections for 30 June 1999)

Assets	$m
Cash	13.0
Intangibles	2.0
Other	1.1
Total assets	**16.1**
Total liabilities	**0.2**
Shareholders' funds	**15.9**

So the public were putting up $15 million to get 36.9 per cent of the company. Allowing for $2 million in float costs, that still represents more than 80 per cent of the company's assets after floating. The existing shareholders are putting up a net $2.9 million in assets and retain majority control. Note that if the $2 million intangibles were stripped out the figures would look even worse.

So were the businesses that were being injected into ChaosMusic profitable? The prospectus showed that in the year to June 1998 they made a profit of $58 000 after tax. In the year to June 1999 they were projected to make a loss of $408 000. To justify their capitalisation of $23 million those businesses would have to start making money very quickly, which they didn't.

It is also worth comparing the market capitalisation of the proposed company against the size of the market which it is aiming to capture. The prospectus said that online music sales (which would be ChaosMusic's main business) were expected to reach $15 million in 1999. Even if it were growing rapidly (which ChaosMusic expected) that was not a large number compared to ChaosMusic's proposed capitalisation of $40 million.

One other negative point about ChaosMusic was that it was being floated by bookbuild. Following the success of the float of the first tranche of Telstra, bookbuilds were quite popular in Australia by 1999. However, they have two disadvantages for subscribers. The first is that subscribers don't know how much they will have to pay for shares until the eve of listing. They're buying into the float blind. The second is that in an old-fashioned float, subscribers buy shares at a set price and if there is any enthusiasm for the company it will be demonstrated after listing as buyers bid for the stock. In a bookbuild, at least some of that enthusiasm is absorbed in the float auction process which usually means there will be comparatively less enthusiasm after listing. This occurred with ChaosMusic, whose shares rarely traded above issue price in the first six months after listing.

Let's take another example, this time from the world of mining. In 1998, a prospectus was released for the proposed float of Silver Rose Mining NL. The structure of the offer is set out in Table 5.3.

148 THE NUMBERS GAME

Table 5.3 Silver Rose proposed float

Party	No. of shares	Cost ($)	%	Capitalis-ation ($)
Seed capitalists and promoters	45 600 005	293 201	53.3	9 120 000
Public	40 000 000	8 000 000	46.7	8 000 000
Total	**85 600 005**	**8 293 201**	**100.0**	**17 120 000**

After the float, Silver Rose would own a bunch of mineral leases scattered across Western Australia and South Australia. They were mainly prospective for silver. Some exploration work had been done on them by prior holders, but the promoters of Silver Rose had spent relatively little on them. The balance sheet of Silver Rose shown in the prospectus revealed that a total of $423 553 had been spent on the leases by the promoters and seed capitalists. They had subscribed $293 201 in capital to Silver Rose and provided it with loans of another $269 043.

It didn't take a Rhodes scholar to appraise this one. The promoters and seed capitalists were proposing to take 53 per cent of the company in return for expenditure of $293 201 (the loans would have been repaid from the float proceeds), while the public were being asked to stump up $8 million for 47 per cent.

The float was abandoned. However, one point should be noted in Silver Rose's favour. At least the promoters were prepared to declare in the prospectus how much they had spent on the leases they were selling to the public. In my opinion, that disclosure should be mandatory in all mining prospectuses.

Will the company have enough money to achieve its objectives?

If the vendors rip enough out, the company will be left high and dry. Laurie Connell floated Vital Technology Australia Ltd in 1985 to raise some $9.9 million from the public. The asset was some image-based information systems and a fiche pack owned by a partnership called WA High Technology Ventures. The partnership took 20 million shares in Vital Technology as a vendor consideration plus $3.5 million cash.

That left Vital Technology with $6.4 million. From that, $3.5 million was paid to another company to 'finance the development of a production model of the prototype'. The issue cost $700 000, which meant only $2.2 million was left to develop and market this gee-whiz technology. Even in the mid-1980s this didn't look like a lot of money. Vital Technology was a dog and went down in flames with the rest of the Connell empire. Any critical reader of the prospectus could have forecast its future.

Are there related party contracts?

Up front in the prospectus is GlossyLand, full of breathtaking photos and visuals of the company's Star Wars technology or other exciting assets. Down the back end of the document is (or should be) some very fine, dense print detailing the company's material contracts. Sometimes a magnifying glass is necessary to read this stuff, but amongst it should be any contracts with related parties, including the directors.

It's a black mark for any company if the directors are going to be charging ongoing consultancy fees. The whole purpose of having a director is for him or her to give the board their best advice. They already collect directors' fees for that. If they are getting consultancy fees as well, they're double-dipping.

PREJUDICE 29

Directors who charge consultancy fees—or commissions— are looking after their own enrichment, not that of the shareholders.

And (a laughable question in the dotcom boom) does the company have any earnings? Or even revenue?

If a product or service is only an idea—a glint in some promoter's eye—it's really worth nothing yet and should be valued as such.

The same principles hold for mining exploration stocks, where the assets will commonly be bits of ground which some geologist thinks are prospective. Check whether the directors are

150 THE NUMBERS GAME

experienced in mining and have a track record of success. Try to check how much the prospects cost the vendors, including any exploration work on them, and compare that with the amount the vendors are charging.

PREJUDICE 30

Beware of hockey sticks.

Take the back of the nearest envelope and draw a graph of the following numbers:

1 last year's loss, $1 million;
2 this year's loss, $900 000;
3 next year's profit (after the float), $5 million.

Figure 5.1 The hockey stick

If you see one of these in a prospectus, run in the other direction

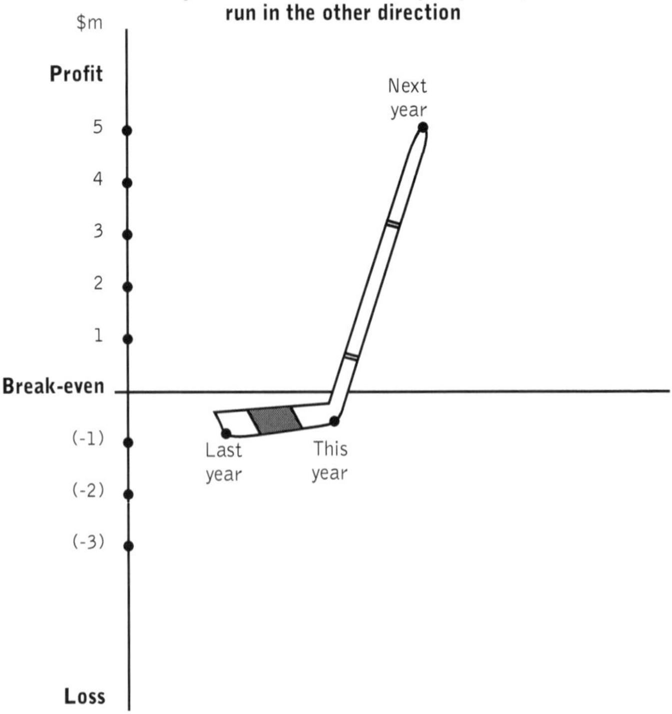

$m

Profit

5

4

3

2

1

Break-even

(-1)   Last   This
        year   year

(-2)

(-3)

Next
year

Loss

What you have drawn is a hockey stick (Figure 5.1). When chief executive of Consolidated Press, Al Dunlap always used to swear to executives: 'I never wanna see a goddam hockey stick company'. A hockey stick is one which performed poorly last year and will perform poorly this year but—after you have invested a heap of money in it—is magically going to perform spectacularly next year. Prospectuses are the natural habitat of hockey stick companies. Take a very quizzical look at the forecasts and decide whether they are reasonable. It's amazing how often they're not.

6

Takeovers

Takeover bids may be divided into two types: hostile and friendly. They may be further divided into two other types: those which have an all-cash alternative and those which don't.

> ## PREJUDICE 31
>
> A bid which is hostile to directors may be quite friendly to shareholders.

Hostile bids

A hostile takeover bid is not necessarily a disaster for shareholders in the target company. When AMP Ltd raided GIO it eventually cranked the bid up to $5.35 a share. Judging by the subsequent disastrous write-offs in GIO's reinsurance business, that may have been about $5.35 more than the company was worth. (For more about this disaster, see under 'General insurance' in Chapter 3.) Nevertheless GIO's board defended the company vigorously, urging shareholders not to sell. Those who ignored the board and took the cash were the sensible ones. The 43 per cent of GIO shareholders who held out were eventually forced to accept a considerably lower paper bid from AMP. Their alternative would have been to dig deep and refinance GIO themselves.

This bid contained many valuable lessons for shareholders.

The main one is that it is highly dangerous to launch a hostile bid for a financial institution.

The accounts of banks and insurance companies are difficult to analyse for experts, as well as lay investors. They can contain quite large, unseen liabilities. GIO's contained real monsters in its reinsurance division. A friendly bid would have enabled AMP to do a due diligence on the GIO accounts and become aware of the lurking dangers. If AMP could not make a friendly bid—and the hostility between the two parties probably meant it would always be impossible—they should have walked away rather than persist with a hostile bid, which turned out to be the worst single disaster in AMP's long history.

Hostile bids can be good news for shareholders. A hostile raider will tend to pitch its bid higher than a friendly one might. Directors of the target company, faced with a hostile bid, might scout around to find an alternative bidder. There is always a chance that an auction will begin and when corporate raiders start competing in an auction one or more of them is always liable to bid more than the target company is worth. In 1989, a duel developed between Abe Goldberg and John Spalvins for control of Industrial Equity Limited (IEL) which culminated in Spalvins' Adelaide Steamship group buying IEL for $1.7 billion. That was nearly double what IEL later proved to be worth.

PREJUDICE 32

In takeovers, cash is king.

Another factor in favour of hostile takeovers from a shareholders' perspective is that a hostile raider often has to offer cash. It's relatively difficult for a hostile raider to force his company's scrip on to target shareholders.

Cash is beautifully uncomplicated. It can be counted and compared to the last sale price of the target stock. It can be banked and reinvested in some other company.

Scrip, by contrast, comes with a few problems. The first requirement is to analyse the raider's accounts and decide whether the shares represent a good investment. The acid test is

154 THE NUMBERS GAME

the question: 'Would I invest in this company at this price?' The answer will tell you whether you should accept scrip or not.

Friendly bids

Friendly bids are not necessarily friendly to shareholders, but at least the two companies have an opportunity to do a proper due diligence on each other and work out whether there will be genuine synergies in a merger.

Sometimes it's win-win. The Tabcorp bid for Star City was all scrip but few shareholders could have complained about the outcome, at least in the medium term.[1] Star City had been underperforming, but after the bid its shareholders had a stake both in Sydney's casino and the Melbourne TAB and gaming business—two of the best gaming franchises in Australia. Star City's results began improving almost immediately.

PREJUDICE 33

Friendly takeovers may not be friendly for shareholders.

In hostile takeovers the air is loud with the din of battle. The two sides may descend to personal insults and newspaper advertising to try to win the fight. Friendly takeovers, by contrast, are very cosy affairs. Sometimes they're a good deal for shareholders, but sometimes they're just too cosy.

The friendly takeovers that should be regarded with the most suspicion are those where the directors or major shareholders have a foot in both camps. One of the classics in this respect was the takeover of Western United by Kia Ora Gold in 1987.

Kia Ora had struck it lucky with the Marvel Loch goldmine near Southern Cross in Western Australia, which it sold to Mawson Pacific for $66 million. As a result of the sale, Kia Ora had net assets of $68 million, most of it in cash. This should have been a bonanza for shareholders, who could legitimately have expected directors to make a return of capital. Instead, the directors decided to take over Western United, a Perth-based financial services group in which Kia Ora's directors held a 33 per cent stake. The bid was announced on 13 October, barely three weeks after the sale of Marvel Loch.

Even at the time it appeared that Western United was being overpriced, which meant that Western United shareholders were getting a better deal than Kia Ora's. The two alternative bids by Kia Ora offered mixtures of shares and cash with a market value ranging from $85 million to $100 million. That represented a huge premium on Western United's market capitalisation of $60 million. As Western United had reported a profit of $1.7 million in 1987, the offers also represented P/E ratios ranging from 50 to 59 times. Also, Western United had only $5 million in tangible assets. So by any conventional measure it was a very expensive purchase. Nevertheless, a shareholders' meeting approved the bid, so it went ahead.

The takeover had hardly been completed when it was followed by a second in May 1988. In the second takeover, Kia Ora bought a string of companies from Duke Holdings Ltd for $12.25 million cash and the issue of 99.4 million shares. Kia Ora also assumed Duke liabilities totalling $28 million.

Both of these takeovers proved a dreadful waste of Kia Ora's money. Duke collapsed in 1989 and the directors who were responsible for the deals spent years fighting court cases.

What should shareholders do when faced by what looks like an awful takeover? Let's say all goes sour. You are a shareholder in a company that is facing a takeover which looks awful. There's no cash alternative and it's all scrip. The best response is to head for the exit and sell the shares on market. You probably won't get much of a price for them, but you'll at least retrieve something and live to invest another day. It's pretty sad being locked into a stock you hate. Life's too short.

Loyalty

Alert readers may have wondered about a missing word in this section—loyalty. Loyalty is one of humanity's most admirable qualities. It is essential in marriages, armies and dogs.

Shareholders often develop strong loyalties for companies. In a hostile takeover battle, the directors will often call on those loyalties—exhorting shareholders to rally round the flag and stand firm against the foe. Stirring stuff, and it often works with small shareholders. However, most share registers are dominated by institutions and professional investors, who take a much colder attitude towards money. Once they decide to sell out, the game's over.

There's not much future standing alone with your musket once the fort has fallen. You're only going to get run over by a tank. Sell your stock and head for the hills. You'll find another company somewhere else and in time you may even grow to love it as much as your old one.

PREJUDICE 34

Save your loyalty for your football team. In the stock market it can be not only misplaced, but expensive.

7

A few danger signals

There is literally no limit to the number and variety of reefs and rocks an investor can hit while sailing the treacherous investment seas. Here are just a few eclectic danger signals that may help avoid a shipwreck.

Has the company been doing back-to-back loans just before balance date?

This is a highly dangerous form of window-dressing. Unfortunately it is nearly always done so that it will be (deliberately) invisible to even an expert reader of the accounts. In the 1980s, Rothwells and the Spedley group used to do extensive back-to-backs with each other to conceal the growing losses in their accounts. An example of a back-to-back (sometimes called Brigitte Bardots) can be taken from the 1984 accounts of Rothwells.

L.R. Connell & Partners (LRC&P), the family company of the chief executive, Laurie Connell, had debts totalling a staggering $34 million to Rothwells. Just before Rothwells balance date in 1984 the debts disappeared, largely through round-robins. Rothwells loaned money to Spedley companies, which loaned it to LRC&P. The disappearance of the debts was therefore financed by Rothwells itself. Immediately after balance date the transactions were reversed and LRC&P went on to incure ever greater debts to Rothwells over the next four years. Neither the Rothwell or Spedley accounts ever gave any clue that these transactions were happening.

157

158 THE NUMBERS GAME

Do companies in a group engage in substantial financial intercourse with each other?

Where such related party transactions are visible and substantial, they should set off instant alarm bells. The companies are tacitly admitting that the only way they can make profits is by dealing with each other rather than the world at large. They are the strongest indication of a looming disaster and, quite possibly, fraud.

Is there a dominant chief executive?

Where the chairman or chief executive is also the major shareholder there is always a danger he or sometimes she will do deals that are in their own interests as opposed to those of the company. The classic case was Alan Bond. His conviction in the La Promenade case was for putting his interests ahead of those of his public company. There were several other deals where Bond exhibited the same behaviour.

Are this year's accounts comparable with last year's?

Does the company keep tinkering with its structure so that it is difficult to get a line on its true performance and there seems no good reason for the changes?

In the early 1970s the Ipec group of Gordon Barton never seemed to manage to produce two successive sets of comparable accounts. The parent company, Ipec Transport, owned about 49.99 per cent of Ipec Insurance, so it wasn't consolidated. Then next year, Ipec Transport bought a couple of hundred shares in Ipec Insurance and consolidated it. That threw the numbers out considerably because Ipec Insurance was larger than Ipec Transport. There was a suspicion that if the insurance arm did well it would be consolidated but if it did poorly it would be deconsolidated. By the time the third year rolled around I had kept the accounts from the two previous years so I was ready to make comparisons whether the insurance company was in or out of the group. But then Ipec Transport changed its balance date and I couldn't compare them anyway. It was all too hard to understand and the best advice to investors is to just stay away from any group that's forever shuffling around like that.

What is the exposure to joint ventures?

I have seen a property company with only a couple of million dollars in shareholders' funds show a joint venture in its accounts as a $1 asset when that joint venture had exposures large enough to bring the parent company into liquidation, which it did. So always try to analyse your company's actual exposure to joint ventures.

If a substantial subsidiary or associate has been taken off the balance sheet, has the exposure been fully disclosed?

The example that comes to mind is CSR's treatment of Delhi Petroleum in the 1970s. They took it off balance sheet—through a trust structure—to keep their gearing down. But as they then disclosed the basic financing of the trust every analyst simply added the lot back onto their balance sheet and they gained nothing from the exercise. It was all pretty futile.

There is more room for distrust where a large entity is lurking off the balance sheet, not consolidated and not fully disclosed.

This goes in spades where the associated company or joint venture or even subsidiary is a financier of some kind. Elders never consolidated Elders Finance although they did give a skeletal balance sheet for it in their notes to accounts. But Elders was always reticent about the manifest disasters in Elders Finance. What went wrong there was never explained.

PREJUDICE 35

If a company is unwilling to talk about an off-balance-sheet entity, shareholders are entitled to assume it's bad news.

160 THE NUMBERS GAME

Are there signs of debt defeasance among the liabilities?

Hooker Corporation inflated its 1987 shareholders' funds and profit by indulging in a *debt defeasance*—a piece of financial engineering aimed at artificially reducing liabilities. It takes several forms, but is most simply described as a book entry which treats borrowings as having been discharged after interest-earning investments are placed in a trust established with the agreement of creditors to pay out the borrowings as they fall due.

The 1987 Hooker accounts showed a leap in shareholders' funds from $270 million to $450 million. The main reason for this surge was a mystic item which had suddenly appeared in the accounts—a 'deferred profits' of $159 million. Notes to the accounts were enigmatic, but they showed that $141 million of the figure arose from 'profit arising from a liability assumption agreement which will be emerged [sic] over the next 10 years'. It took an inquiry by the National Corporations and Securities Commission (NCSC) to establish what had happened.[1]

An overseas subsidiary of Hooker had borrowed US$165 million from a US bank for ten years. After a series of transactions, including the deposit of US$63 million in a sinking fund for the benefit of the bank and the exchange of interest obligations by the subsidiary and a second bank, the subsidiary was legally released from its principal and interest obligations under the original loan. Hooker's view was that the cash surplus arising of US$102 million (then A$141 million) was not required to be repaid but bore a servicing cost, net of hedging, of about 8 per cent over the ten years. To put it another way, Hooker had arranged a long-term loan which was immediately repaid on a discounted net present value basis, plus a servicing fee which equated to the interest rate. After inspecting the transaction the NCSC concluded there was a $30 million profit arising, but the remaining $111 million, representing the servicing fee, was a liability and ought to have been represented as such in the accounts. But that ignored the true purposes of this piece of financial engineering. If Hooker had shown the $111 million as a liability instead of an asset it would have been in breach of its negative pledge borrowing covenants. The artificiality of the whole deal was exposed a couple of years later when Hooker hit the wall and it became clear that what Hooker had was a liability, warts and all.

It's pretty complex, but the message is clear. Be very wary if the word 'defeasance' ever crops up anywhere in the accounts.

Are balance sheet figures netted out?

An example is Chase Corporation's 1988 balance sheet (summarised in Table 7.1).

Table 7.1 Summary of Chase Corporation's balance sheet, 1988

	NZ$m
Total assets	2 824
Total liabilities	(1 681)
Shareholders' funds	1 143

Not too bad. Gearing a little high at nearly 60 per cent. But just a second! On the asset side there was a line 'Net Investments in Finance, Non and Limited Recourse Property Group, $127 million'. What did they mean—'Net'?

In the notes to accounts it was revealed that Chase had netted out some of the liabilities on the grounds they were non-recourse. That $127 million represented the difference between $470 million in property assets and $343 million in property borrowings.

If they had been added back on each side of the equation, we would have had total assets of $3167 million and total liabilities of $2024 million. Gearing has suddenly swung up to 64 per cent. It may well have been that the loans were truly against the projects with no recourse against the group. However, by netting out the figure in the balance sheet Chase was giving an illusory picture of its assets. That $127 million was not 100 per cent of an asset—it was 27 per cent. To put it another way, a 27 per cent fall in the project values would have wiped it out entirely, which is what eventually happened.

Does the little word 'net' occur in the extraordinaries?

It always pays to take a close look at those notes to the accounts relating to the profit, and particularly any notes on the extraordinaries. This is where the occasional clue can be found that a monster is lurking. Take the 1984 profit and loss account of CSR (Table 7.2).

Table 7.2 Profit and loss account for CSR, 1984

	$m
EBIT	218.7
Interest	(58.3)
Tax	(57.1)
Minorities	(0.3)
Net profit	91.7
Net extraordinaries	0.3
Profit after extras	92.0

There were a couple of things wrong with this so-called profit. At this time CSR had shuffled Delhi Petroleum off balance sheet into a fund in which it held just under 50 per cent. That fund reported a $2 million profit for the year after incurring, but not paying, an interest bill of $80 million. If it had been consolidated and the interest had not been capitalised, therefore, CSR's profit would have been something like $50 million instead of $92 million.[2]

But there's also that little word 'net' again. Note 7 to the accounts revealed that the little surplus of $0.3 million shown as an extraordinary gain was actually the resultant of 21 separate line items. They are summarised in Table 7.3.

So! Our net extraordinaries of a mere $320 000 turn out to be the difference of a total of $95.1 million in extraordinary gains and $94.8 million in losses. The company had taken huge losses, particularly in its concrete and quarrying businesses, which had not been recognised for several years. Now it had recognised them, it balanced the account by selling its historic head office at 1 O'Connell Street. That's the $59 million profit in the first line.

Table 7.3 CSR's 1984 extraordinaries

	$m
Surplus on disposal of land and buildings	59.1
Additional proceeds from previous sales of oil and gas interests	14.9
Income tax benefit	19.3
Other extraordinary gains	1.8
Losses on sale of significant business segments	(11.3)
Provision for loss on sale of significant business segments	(7.6)
Provision for diminution in value of significant business segments	(19.2)
Write-down of fixed assets in anticipation of loss on sale	(25.1)
Adjustments arising from irregularities in Ready Mixed Farley since 1981 and associated costs	(20.5)
Other extraordinary losses	(11.1)
Total net extraordinaries	**0.3**

Instead of a steady-as-she-goes result, you have something that really leaves you worrying about the management of the company. What had happened was not adequately explained anywhere in the annual report. CSR's losses in concrete and quarrying had been so large they had to sell the head office to cover the hole. Even worse, it later turned out they hadn't sold the head office at all. It had been shuffled off balance sheet and wasn't sold for another three years. If you dig through the notes to the 1987 accounts you'll find the eventual sale.

And note the $19.3 million in future tax benefits. If we knock them out of the stated profit, and take into account that the head office wasn't actually sold, CSR in truth made a large loss in 1984.

Are the assets really worth what the company says?

Commonsense will take you a long way. The best test for any asset value is to ask: 'How much could I sell it for?' If it's past advertising expenditure, my answer would be zero. If dividends are being paid out of revaluations of properties that have not been sold, ask yourself what will happen on the inevitable day when prices go down again. The answer is pretty obvious, but was missed by a whole generation of company directors in the 1970s and 1980s. None so blind as those who don't want to see.

Is the market saying the same thing as the company?

Keep one eye on the accounts but the other on the share market. If a company is saying one thing (that it's sound and profitable) while the market is saying another (the share price keeps sliding), then always, *always* believe the market.

Do the revenue figures in the cash flow statement look anything like the revenue figures in the profit and loss account?

If they're within, say, 10 per cent of each other, the explanation is probably timing differences or some technical factor. If the revenue figures in the profit and loss account are much higher than those in the cash flow statement, the company is probably front-end loading. It's taking into account (and profit) sales revenue that won't be received until some time after balance date. Maybe years after balance date and maybe never.

8

Fixed interest (boring but essential)

Any properly constructed investment portfolio should contain an element of fixed interest investments, usually amounting to about one-third of the total. Fixed interest is normally regarded as the boring bit, although it can be exciting enough when monetary policy goes out of whack.

The inverse correlation

The most fundamental point to understand about fixed interest is the inverse correlation between price and yield. Let's say Sir Mark Time, the boneheaded chairman of Blue Sky Mines NL, invests $1000 in a Commonwealth bond with a coupon rate of 5 per cent maturing in ten years time. This is a capital guaranteed investment which means that if Sir Mark hangs on to the bond for the full ten years he will get his $1000 back. Meanwhile it will yield him interest at a deeply unexciting $50 a year.

Now let's say that a year after Sir Mark bought his bond, the Reserve Bank doubles interest rates from 5 per cent to 10 per cent. (They haven't done anything that extreme in recent years, although in the mid-1970s they came close.) Nobody is going to pay $1000 for his 5 per cent bond when they can now invest $1000 in a bond that will yield them 10 per cent. So if Sir Mark wants to sell his bond in the secondary market before maturity, the price will be adjusted to reflect the current yield rate of

165

166 THE NUMBERS GAME

10 per cent. For his $50 annual interest payment to represent a yield of 10 per cent, simple arithmetic tells us the bond will have to be priced at $500. Actually it won't be that low because the bond dealers would take into account the fact that a capital profit would accrue upon maturity and they would factor that in to calculate what is called a yield to redemption. The true price would therefore only slump to about $550, but Sir Mark will still have lost nearly half his investment—if he wants to cash in the bond.

At the risk of repetition, let's restate the lesson. Bond prices and yields are inverse to each other. A rise in interest rates will depress bond prices; a fall in interest rates will lift bond prices.

Note that if Sir Mark's bond is held through to maturity, there will be no loss of capital. Sir Mark will instead be accepting a substandard rate of return for all those years. In some institutional accounts, bonds and other fixed interest securities have to be marked-to-market each year whether there is any intention to sell them or not. So if Sir Mark's bond was held by, say, AMP Ltd the annual accounts would show that it was losing $450 on the investment. But as long as the intention is to hold the bond to maturity, it's only a paper loss.

The closer the bond gets to maturity, the closer its market price will converge to its value upon maturity. This is true whether interest rates rise or fall during the currency of the bond.

Okay? Now let's look at where interest rates have been for the past quarter of a century (Table 8.1).

It may help understanding of the table to point out that Australia had not seen double-digit official interest rates in the twentieth century until the Labor Party pushed them through 10 per cent in 1974. So Table 8.1 begins in a period where interest rates were rising strongly. Once interest rates had been cranked to that level, it took seventeen years to get them back to single digits again. The old saying about interest rates is that they go up in the elevator but come down by the stairs.

Bond rates have been chosen because they are the best indicator of what was happening in the economy as a whole. Readers may assume that other rates, such as those offered by banks and finance companies, maintained a more or less constant margin above the bond rates.

In 1976, the gap between three- and ten-year bond rates was

Table 8.1 Australian interest rates 1976–99

Year[a]	2 and 3 year bonds[b] %	5 year bonds %	10 year bonds %
1976	8.5	9.4	10.0
1977	9.9	10.2	10.4
1978	8.8	9.1	9.1
1979	9.9	10.0	10.0
1980	11.5	11.8	11.8
1981	13.2	13.1	13.1
1982	16.4	16.4	16.4
1983	13.7	14.3	14.7
1984	12.2	13.0	13.7
1985	13.4	13.3	13.5
1986	12.8	12.8	12.9
1987	13.0	13.1	12.8
1988	11.7	11.9	11.9
1989	15.4	14.2	13.5
1990	14.0	13.8	13.4
1991	10.5	11.1	11.2
1992	7.0	7.8	8.9
1993	6.2	6.8	7.4
1994	8.6	9.0	9.6
1995	8.3	8.6	9.2
1996	8.3	8.6	8.9
1997	5.9	6.4	7.0
1998	5.2	5.4	5.6
1999	5.6	5.9	6.3
2000	5.9	6.0	6.2
2001	5.3	5.8	6.0
2002	5.4	5.8	6.0

Source: Reserve Bank of Australia

Notes: [a] Prevailing rates in June each year

[b] Two-year bond rates to 1992, three-year rates thereafter

nominally 1.5 per cent. However an investor in a ten-year bond would have been receiving 17 per cent more dollars than an investor in a three-year bond. The only year in which the nominal gap was greater was 1992, when it was 1.9 per cent, and the investor in a ten-year bond would have received 27 per cent more income than anyone in a three-year bond.

For most of the years between 1978 and 1991 the yield spectrum was flat and in some years it was negative, with short-dated bonds yielding more than long-dated bonds. This was an abnormal period because we are talking about years when official interest rates were at historically high levels, but some lessons can be drawn from them for the future, irrespective of where the level of interest rates may go.

1   In a period when interest rates are rising, it pays to stay short. An investor who put all the fixed interest money into ten-year bonds at 10 per cent in 1976 would have done well in the short term, but would also have been locked in until 1986. Short-term investors reaped some high rewards from 1980 onwards.

2   When rates are falling it pays to go long. The peak 16.4 per cent of the 1982 credit squeeze was a good rate even by the exorbitant standards of the 1980s which followed. Investors taking the long-term rates in 1990 or 1991 would also have done comparatively well.

3   If you don't know which way rates are going, you might as well stay short. At least staying short gives you liquidity in that you have the opportunity of reinvesting within a relatively short span, whereas if you make an error in the long term you can be stuck with it for a decade. When rates are low and flat, as they were in 1998, there is almost no incentive to go long term.

Who is the guarantor?

When deciding to make a fixed interest investment, the first question to ask is: Who is ultimately guaranteeing that you are going to get repaid? The Australian Government has never defaulted on an obligation and no state or territory government has defaulted since Jack Lang was running New South Wales in the 1930s (and even then the Commonwealth picked up the tab).

So government securities (bonds and Treasury bills) are regarded as the ultimate safe haven.

Indeed, Commonwealth bonds are the benchmark fixed interest security. If Commonwealth bonds are selling at 6 per cent, it would take a fairly silly investor to make an alternative fixed interest investment at 6 per cent or less. Alternative investments would need to be priced at a margin above 6 per cent to compensate the investor for the extra risk, however slight, of lending money elsewhere.

So that's another inverse correlation in fixed interest: the safer the investment the lower the rate, and vice versa. Any outfit offering high interest rates and promising perfect safety is either stupid or dishonest. The higher the rate, the higher the risk.

Ignore that maxim at your peril. The classic case in recent years was the Estate Mortgage group of trusts in the 1980s, which employed quite unscrupulous advertising to persuade investors that they were safe when in fact they were becoming progressively less safe. That crash caused more anguish among small investors than almost any other collapse of the 1980s.

Australian banks are pretty safe. No depositor in an Australian bank has lost money in nearly 70 years. There is no absolute guarantee that this safety will persist, but it's not a bad bet. So loans to banks or purchases of bank bills are safe enough investments. Note that bank's subsidiaries are not always guarantored by them. This became an issue in the late 1980s when it looked as though some bank finance subsidiaries might hit the wall. In any future crisis the banks probably would bail out their subsidiaries but we can't be totally sure.

Not every security issued by a government or bank can be regarded as having equal safety. The governments of major westernised countries have a good modern record of honouring their obligations, but governments in the underdeveloped world have a deservedly riskier reputation. South American countries have a long and consistent history of loan defaults going back to the early nineteenth century (yet they still seem to catch Americans by surprise about once a decade). Russia defaulted on its bonds in 1998.

Big, well-known foreign banks should be safe, but there is no shortage of dodgy banks around the world. Russia's chief

170 THE NUMBERS GAME

prosecutor, Yuri Skuratov, has been reported as saying that half that country's banks are controlled by the Russian Mafia.[1] The Bank of Credit and Commerce International had a resounding enough name until it collapsed in 1992. Then it earned the reputation of being the world's sleaziest bank, deeply enmeshed in money laundering, corruption and drug dealing. (Come to think of it, a drug dealing bank should be a surefire profitmaker, but somehow BCCI wasn't.)

There is an enormous array of fixed interest securities on offer to investors even without straying beyond Australia's shores. The following list has been supplied by Sydney dealer Lewis Securities.

- *Bonds*—issued by borrowers such as the Commonwealth Government and semi-government authorities. These borrowers guarantee their bonds. The bonds pay a fixed rate of interest and mature at a fixed point in time.
- *Bank bills*—a bank bill is a non-interest paying security. It is sold at a discount to face value so that the investor receives all the proceeds at maturity. Bank bills can be bought for amounts from $50 000 and are highly liquid. They are issued on terms of 30 days up to 180 days.
- *Debentures*—sometimes called corporate bonds, these are typically issued by large companies or finance companies, which guarantee them, in return for medium to long-term investment of funds up to five years.
- *Bank bonds*—transferable deposit securities issued and guaranteed by banks. These have many of the features of debentures, although at a higher security level.
- *Inflation (CPI)-indexed bonds*—bonds issued by the government in which the value of interest payments and the capital value of the bond on maturity are not fixed when the bonds are issued. Instead they are linked or indexed to the inflation rate as measured by the CPI.
- *Inflation-indexed annuities*—bonds issued by governments, authorities and major companies in which investors receive quarterly payments, indexed by CPI inflation, throughout the term but at maturity there is no residual. Each payment therefore comprises partial return of the capital, interest and

inflation components. These annuity bonds are used to finance infrastructure projects such as tollways and are suitable investments for allocated pension funds.

- *Term deposits*—offered by banks for set periods at fixed rates. Unlike the other securities in this list, these cannot be traded on a secondary market. They enjoy a high safety rating, but are illiquid for most practical purposes.
- *Income securities*—issued by banks and financial institutions. The interest rate on these securities is a fixed margin over the bank bill rate. They therefore offer a better return than the prevailing bill rate. The downside is that maturity is at the option of the issuer. They may therefore never mature, and the only way a holder may cash them is on the secondary market. The trap is that if a holder buys an income security yielding 1 per cent over bill rates, and some rival institution issues income securities yielding 2 per cent over, then the price of the first issuer's income securities will go to a discount relative to the second.
- *Hybrid securities*—come in a wide range of varieties but typically are convertible or resettable preference shares. In a typical case a resettable pref will have a yield which is at a given margin of, say, 2 per cent above the bank bill rate. The rate can be reset at some date in the future, maybe five years after issue. At the reset date, there is usually an option to convert into shares of the issuing company, or in some cases to redeem for cash. The buyer is being offered a fixed interest return with a potential equity kicker. There are three points to be taken into consideration. 1. Who is the guarantor of ultimate repayment (sometimes these securities are not issued by the company into which the shares will finally convert)? 2. Is the company in which you will ultimately be holding shares sound? 3. Does the interest rate margin offer sufficient compensation for risk?

Ratings

Professional fixed interest analysts spend a lot of time studying the soundness of issuers. Many institutions are compelled by their trust deeds to invest only in what are called investment grade securities. Investment grade depends on individual definition, but broadly it would comprise any issuer with an A rating from the credit agencies plus any Australian banks.

Moody's Investor Services and Standard & Poor are the world's leading rating agencies. In recent years their ratings have developed the status of Holy Writ. But, as ever, there is room for cynicism.

In August 1994 Moody's gave Orange County's debt a rating of Aa1, the highest of any California county. A cover memo to the rating letter said: 'Well done, Orange County'. On 5 December, barely three months later, Orange County filed the largest municipal bankruptcy petition in history. The losses amounted to almost $1000 for every man, woman and child in the county. On 7 December, a deeply embarrassed Moody's declared Orange County's bond to be 'junk'. Standard & Poor had also failed to anticipate the bankruptcy.

So much for rating agencies.

Epilogue

Money is at some degree of risk whatever you do with it. A miser who keeps cash under his mattress or in a teapot in the backyard risks losing it to a burglar.

An investor in government bonds has safeguarded his nominal capital, but inflation may ravage its value while it is tied up. A buyer of equities will inevitably see them fluctuate in value.

There is no totally safe area.

The best an investor can do is to try to ensure that his ultimate reward from an investment is commensurate with the degree of risk he or she is taking. This is made more difficult by the fact that every other investor is simultaneously trying to do the same.

An honest advisor, who is also smart, is an investor's best asset.

The investment world is a jungle, but once an investor knows the habits of the animals and how to read their signs by following the numbers game, his chances of survival are greatly improved. But there's still no such thing as perfect safety.

As the desk sergeant used to say in *Hill Street Blues*—'Be careful out there.'

Notes

1 Investment basics

1 The ranking of the Australian Taxation Office is a little better than it appears. If a company has not been paying its PAYE taxes, the ATO has the power to hold the directors personally liable. Therefore all but the most stupid directors make sure that their PAYE instalments are up to date. For other taxes such as PAYG and company tax, the ATO ranks with unsecured creditors.

2 The title of the ASIC guide is 'Don't Kiss Your Money Goodbye'. The web address is www.asic.gov.au.

3 The numbers are from ASIC's FIDO managed fee calculator. A management fee in a fund or trust would have precisely the same effect.

2 Basic analysis

1 Definitions of ordinary, abnormal and extraordinary profits as given by J.B. & M.A. Shanahan, *Guide to Accounting Standards*, Deloitte Touche Tohmatsu, 1997. This excellent work is updated annually by the authors and is an authoritative guide to the latest changes in accounting standards.

2 If you want to get technical, the calculation should also include 6.3 million partly paid shares (also called contributing shares) issued under Amcor's employee share plan. Adding them on to Amcor's fully paid shares gives a total of 638.5 million shares on issue. But when doing this, you should also add to

shareholders' funds the amount still to be paid on the shares, which was $50.7 million. That would give us net assets of $2774.4 million divided by 638.5 million, which is a NAB of $4.34 per share.

If a company has options on issue, the same calculation applies. Add the number of options to the issued capital (first checking whether the options convert into shares on a 1:1 basis) and add the exercise price to the net assets. Then you have what is called the *net asset backing on a fully diluted basis*. The company's forecast earnings per share can also be adjusted by using this fully diluted basis.

Note, however, that the calculation is only valid as long as the options or partly paid shares are in the money. The amount due on the Amcor contributing shares was $7.95 a share. As that was pretty close to Amcor's market price at the time the accounts were issued, it would be valid to include the partly paids in the calculation. But if the conversion price were significantly above market then they should be excluded.

3 It should be pointed out that control and management of Digicall have totally changed since its wild early days.

3 Types of companies

1 David Hale, speech to Australian Gold Conference, Perth, April 1999.

2 Productivity Commission Inquiry Report, 'Australia's Gambling Industries', Appendix U, 1999, p. 4. To put it more accurately, a win rate of 90 per cent means the average loss is 10 per cent of the accumulated amount put through the machine. Hence the longer a player keeps putting his or her money through the machine, the more certain they are to lose.

3 The report of the HIH Royal Commission is entitled 'The Failure of HIH Insurance' and is available in three volumes from government bookshops. Recommendations on changes in the law are found in Volume I.

4 An exceedingly bright analyst might have got an inkling from the fact that between 1997 and 2000, the underwriting result was deteriorating despite an increase in net written premiums. However, this analytical exercise would have been greatly

complicated by the fact that HIH had an 18 month year in 1999 when it changed balance date.

5 Mr Justice Owen's estimate.

6 The table, in extended form, appears on p. 60 of Volume III of the Royal Commission report.

7 An exceedingly bright analyst might have got an inkling from the fact that between 1997 and 2000 the underwriting result was deteriorating despite an increase in net written premiums. However, this analytical exercise would have been greatly complicated by the fact that HIH had an 18 month year in 1999 when it changed balance date.

8 Mr Justice Owen's estimate.

9 The table, in extended form, appears on p. 60 of Volume III of the Royal Commission report.

10 My thanks to Graham Kelly, chief executive of Novogen, for some of the background in this segment.

11 In the Westpac 1999 accounts, the details of the capital adequacy calculation are given in Note 22.

12 For a full account of the bank's horrors in this period, read Edna Carew's *Westpac: The Bank that Broke the Bank*, Doubleday, 1997.

13 Study by Mackenzie & Bilodeau, 1984. Quoted in V. Rudenno, *The Mining Valuation Handbook—for Projects, Companies and Shares*, Wrightbooks, 1998.

14 Trevor Sykes, *The Money Miners*, Wildcat Press, 1978, p. 9.

15 *Australian Securities Markets and their Regulation 1974* (Rate Report), part I, vol. I, p. 281.

16 Trevor Sykes, 'Hedges Won't Hinder Golden Age', *Australian Financial Review*, 9 October 1999.

17 Given the importance of mining and oil to Australia, it is amazing how few books have been written in simple English explaining how prospects and companies are valued. This is the only one I know.

18 Rudenno, V., 1998, *Mining Valuation Handbook—for Projects, Companies and Shares*, p. 46.

19 My thanks to Graham Kelly, chief executive of Novogen, for some of the background in this segment.

5 Prospectuses

1 Trevor Sykes, 'Float Promoters Take the Cream', *Australian Financial Review*, 4 January 2000.

6 Takeovers

1 Tabcorp shares did suffer after the bid, but that was mainly because of fears of additional government regulation or taxation of gaming stocks rather than problems with the Star City merger.

7 A few danger signals

1 This occurred after Professor Bob Walker had alerted the public to the manoeuvre in the *Australian Business Magazine* (*ABM*). See 'Hooker's $141m. Book Exercise', *ABM*, 20 January 1988. Walker was Professor of Accountancy at the University of New South Wales.

2 Taking the $80 million interest as an expense would have boosted the interest bill to $138.3, reducing profit before tax to $80 million. Applying tax to that at the same 35.6 per cent rate which CSR was paying would have reduced net profit to between $51 million and $52 million.

8 Fixed interest

1 Nicholas Dunbar, *Inventing Money: The Story of Long Term Capital Management and the Legends Behind it*, John Wiley & Sons, 2000, p. 200.

Index

abnormals, 15, 16, 18–19, 21
actuaries, 59
Amcor accounts, 16–41
AMP, 44, 60, 71, 89, 152–3
annual report, 14
appraisal value, 65–7
area of closure (oil), 125
Australian Securities & Investments
    Commission (ASIC), 4–5
Australian Financial Review, 135,
    176
Australian shares, 11
Australian Taxation Office, 1, 174
Aztec Exploration, 143

back-to-back loans, 157
bad debt provisions, 93
balance dates, 157
balance sheets, 25–36, 60–7, 91
bank bills, 170
bank bonds, 170
bank deposits, 99
Bank of Credit & Commerce
    International, 170
banks, 89–104
Barings, 104
BHP, 112

biotechs, 127–30
blue sky, 117–18
Bond, Alan, 158
Bond Corp, 33, 36
bond rates, 165–8
bonds, 165–8, 170
bookbuilds, 146, 147
brand names, 31–2
Bre-X Minerals, 105–6
BT Funds Management, 12
Burns Philp & Co., 132
Burns Philp Trustee, 132
Burrill, Geoff, 115
Busang, 105–6

Cameron, Alan, 9
capital asset ratios, 92
capitalisation of expenses, 33
Carew, Edna, 176
cash, 10, 28, 50–1, 117–18, 153
cash flow statement, 36–41, 119,
    164
casinos, 53–6
central estimates, 73
ChaosMusic, 146–7
Chase Corp, 161
Cisco Systems, 44

178

INDEX 179

Coles Myer, 50–3
Colonial Ltd, 44, 69–71, 72
commission, 7–8
Commonwealth Bank, 44
Connell, Laurie, 148–9, 157
consolidated accounts, 65
contributing shares, 143–4
Conzinc Riotinto of Australia
(CRA), 120
cost of production (mining
companies), 118–19
costs, 18
creditors, 2
Crown casino, 55–6
CSR, 159, 162–3, 177
current assets, 28–9
current liabilities, 33
current ratio, 34

debenture holders, 2
debentures, 2, 170
debt defeasance, 160–1
Delhi Petroleum, 159
Deloitte Touche Tohmatsu, ix
depreciation and amortisation,
19–20
derivatives, 99–103
Digicall, 37, 39, 175
discount rates, 63–4, 66
discounted cash flow (DCF),
113
Dividend Fund Inc., 144
dividends, 24
dotcoms, 135
drill stem tests, 124
drilling, minerals, 109–10
drilling, oil, 124–5
DRIP schemes, 25
Duke Holdings, 155

Dunbar, Nicholas, 177
Dunlap, Al, 151

earnings per share, 23
EBIT, 20, 51
EBIT margin, 51
EBITDA, 19, 55
ecorp, 45
Elders Finance, 159
embedded value, 70–1
employees, 1
end game, 12–13
Estate Mortgage group, 6,
132–3
expansion factor (oil), 126
experts, 4–10
exploration, 106–7
extraordinaries, 162–3

FAI, 82–3
Federal Drug Administration
(FDA), 129
Felderhof, Dr John, 105
financial advisors, 5–10
financial performance statement,
25–6
fixed assets, 29–33
fixed interest, 10, 165–72
foreign exchange forwards, 100–3
Foxtel, 43
free capital, 97–8
front-end loading, 39
fund managers, 135–7
funds, 134–7
future tax benefits, 32

gaming companies, 53–8
gaming machines, 56–7
Garretty, Dr Michael, 144

gearing, 27–8
general insurance, 72–89
General Property Trust, 139–40
GIO, 44, 84, 85, 86–9, 152–3
goodwill, 31–2, 80
grind business, 54–5, 58
guarantors, 168–71

Hale, David, 175
Hartley platinum mine, 112
hedging, 120–3
H.G. Palmer, 52–3
high rollers, 55
HIH, 76–84
hockey sticks, 150–1
Hooker Corp., 160–1
HotCopper, 141
hybrid securities, 4, 171
hydrocarbon saturation, 126

IBNER, 74
IBNR, 74
income securities, 171
independent directors, 133
indemnity insurance, 9
inflation-indexed annuities, 170–1
inflation-indexed bonds, 170
information memorandum, 143
instalment receipts, 143–4
Insurance Australia Group (IAG),
    73–4
insurance companies, 58–89
intangibles, 31–2, 80
interest, 20–1; capitalisation of, 20
interest rate swaps, 103–4
interest rates, 165–8
inventories, 28–9
investment strategy, 10–12
investments, 30

Ipec group, 158–9

John Fairfax, 43
joint ventures, 159

Kambalda nickel mine, 107–8, 114
Kia Ora Gold, 154–5

Leeson, Nick, 104
lenders, 1
Lew, Reuben, 134
Lew, Richard, 134
Lewis Securities, 170
life insurance, 60–72
limited liability, 143–4
liquidators, 1
long-tail insurance, 76
loyalty, 155–6

managed investments, 132–4
management expense ratio (MER),
    137
margin on services, 62–3, 67, 69
mark-to-market, 65
Microsoft, 44
mining companies, 104–23
Mining Valuation Handbook,
    123–6, 176
minority interests, 22, 36
Moody's Investor Services, 173
Morgan, Hugh, 116
Mt Todd gold mine, 112
Mt Tom Price iron ore mine, 120

National Indemnity, 82–3
National Mutual, 44
net asset backing, 25
net assets, 25, 35, 64–5
net pay (oil), 125

INDEX **181**

net present value (NPV), 113
Newcrest, 122
News Corp, 43
no liability, 144
non-accrual loans, 96–7
non-current assets, 29–33
non-current liabilities, 34–5
normalising, 56
Normandy Mining, 120–1
note 1, 68–70
noteholders, 2
NPAT, 22

off-balance sheet entities, 159
oil and gas companies, 123–31
oil and gas recovery, 127
oil and gas reserves, 125–6
operating result, 18
Oracle, 44
Orange County, 172
ore grades, 110–11, 115–16
ore resources and reserves, 110–12
other assets, 32–3
outside interests, 22, 35
outstanding claims liability, 60–7
outstanding liabilities, 81–2
Ozemail, 43

Pan Pharmaceuticals, 130
Parbo, Sir Arvi, 114
payout ratio, 24–5
PBL, 43, 45, 56
P/E ratio, 23–4
P/EBIT ratio, 45
P/EBITDA ratio, 45
P/EBITDAM ratio, 46
Pegasus Gold, 112
permeability, 126
pharmaceuticals, 130

policyholders, 64
porosity, 126
portfolio management, 10
Poseidon No Liability, 112
preference shares, 1–3
price/revenue multiple, 46
Productivity Commission, 57, 175
profit and loss accounts, 18–22, 164
profit-to-sales ratio, 50–1
property, plant and equipment, 30–1
property trusts, 10, 137–40
prospectus forecasts, 47
prospectuses, 141–51

Qantas, 44
Qintex, 28

ranking of creditors, 1
rating agencies, 171–2
rebalancing, 11–12
receivables, 28, 30
recovery factor (oil), 126
reinsurance, 82, 85–9
related party transactions, 149
retailers, 50–3
retirement, 12–13
return on assets, 93
risk assessment, 76–84
Rothwells, 157
roulette, 54
Rudenno, Dr Victor, 123–6, 176

sales, 16–17
sales per square metre, 53
salting, 105–6
Shanahan, John, 174
shareholders' funds, 25, 92–3

182 THE NUMBERS GAME

shareholders' rights, 1
short-tail insurance, 76
shrinkage factor (oil), 126
Silver Rose Mining, 147–8
Simons, Paul, 53
solvency reserves, 71–2
Sons of Gwalia, 122
Spedley group, 157
Standard & Poor, 173
Star City, 154, 176
State Bank of South Australia, 133
stock-turn ratio, 29, 51
subordinated securities, 35

Tabcorp, 56, 154, 176
takeovers, 88, 119, 152–6
tax, 22
Telstra, 43, 44, 143–4
term deposits, 171
Tin Australia, 142
TMT companies, 42–50
trailing commission, 7–8
trustees, 132–3

unit trusts, 132–3
unitholders, 132–3
unlimited liability, 144
unsolicited offers, 4
unusuals, 15, 16, 18–19, 21

vendors, 144–5
Vital Technology Australia Ltd, 148–9

wagering, 57–8
Walker, Professor Bob, 177
Western United, 154–5
Westpac, 90–9, 104, 176
win rates, 53–5
Windarra nickel mine, 115, 116
WMC (formerly Western Mining), 113–16
Woolworths, 53
work index (of rocks), 112

yields, 165–6

Printed in Great Britain
by Amazon.co.uk, Ltd.,
Marston Gate.